Learner's Pocket Grammar

John Eastwood

OXFORD
UNIVERSITY PRESS

OXFORD
UNIVERSITY PRESS

Great Clarendon Street, Oxford OX2 6DP

Oxford University Press is a department of the University
of Oxford. It furthers the University's objective of excellence
in research, scholarship, and education by publishing
worldwide in

Oxford New York

Auckland Cape Town Dar es Salaam Hong Kong Karachi
Kuala Lumpur Madrid Melbourne Mexico City Nairobi
New Delhi Shanghai Taipei Toronto

With offices in

Argentina Austria Brazil Chile Czech Republic France
Greece Guatemala Hungary Italy Japan Poland Portugal
Singapore South Korea Switzerland Thailand Turkey
Ukraine Vietnam

AUTHOR'S ACKNOWLEDGEMENTS
*I count myself extremely fortunate that this book has been in the capable
hands of the publishing manager Glynnis Keir, editor Andrew Shouler
and designer Phil Hargraves. I am grateful to all of them.*

Contents

CONTENTS

Infinitive, gerund, and participle

The noun phrase

CONTENTS

Adjectives, adverbs, and prepositions

Main clauses and sub-clauses

CONTENTS

Introduction

Oxford Learner's Pocket Grammar provides a complete, concise overview of English grammar for learners at Intermediate level and above. The book is divided into 180 two-page units. Each unit takes a key topic and explains how the grammar works, and how to use it. Example sentences illustrate the grammar in use, and warn students of common errors to avoid. There are over 150 tips offering guidance on the idiomatic use of English. Extensive cross-referencing allows students to build a full, rich understanding of English grammar, and the content of the units reflects thorough corpus-based research.

The book can be used to complement any English course by offering a quick overview of any troublesome grammar points, and a deeper explanation of the most essential grammar than coursebooks typically have space for. It is ideal for revision for exams, and has been written with the grammar syllabuses of IELTS, FCE, CAE and CPE in mind. *Oxford Learner's Pocket Grammar* corresponds to CEF levels B2, C1 and C2.

Used alongside *Oxford Learner's Pocket Dictionary*, this book offers a complete, pocket-sized English language reference package.

SENTENCE AND TEXT

一 Words and phrases

A There are eight word classes in English, sometimes called 'parts of speech'.

Verb: *be, bring, decide, look, must, take, write*
Noun: *car, dog, idea, London, sadness, time*
Adjective: *big, different, high, natural*
Adverb: *badly, often, probably, soon*
Determiner: *a, every, my, the, this*
Pronoun: *him, myself, something, you*
Conjunction: *and, because, but, if*
Preposition: *at, by, to, with*

B Some words belong to more than one word class. Here are some examples.

promise (verb):
  I **promise** I won't be late.
promise (noun):
  I won't be late and that's a **promise**.

human (noun):
  When did **humans** first land on the moon?
human (adjective):
  We're defending our **human** rights.

that (determiner):
  Look at **that** poster.
that (pronoun):
  This is the car **that** I'd like.
that (conjunction):
  I just know **that** it's true.

C There are five kinds of phrase.

A **verb phrase** has an ordinary
verb. There can also be one or more
auxiliaries in front of the ordinary verb.
*was, arrives, can see, don't know,
have been thinking*

A **noun phrase** (➤ 84) has a noun.
There can also be a determiner and/or
an adjective in front of the noun.
music, some money, a good game

An **adjective phrase** is often just an
adjective. There can also be an adverb of
degree (➤ 127) in front of the adjective.
great, very old, most ridiculous

An **adverb phrase** is often just an
adverb. There can be an adverb of
degree (➤ 127) in front of the adverb.
sometimes, very carefully

A **prepositional phrase** is a
preposition + noun phrase. ➤ 135A–B
on the road, by Friday, for a long time

TIP

In English there are lots of verbs that
we can use as nouns in expressions
such as *have a look*, *make a copy* and
do a search. ➤ 47

∩ **The simple sentence**

These are the possible structures in a simple sentence.

A Subject + Verb
> *The visitors have arrived.*
> *The old man died.*

A verb in this structure is called an intransitive verb, e.g. *arrive, die, rise, wait.*

B Subject + Verb + Object
> *The kids have eaten all the sandwiches.*
> *The shop sells computers.*

A verb in this structure is called a transitive verb, e.g. *eat, sell, take, wear.*

C Subject + Verb + Complement
> *This jacket is nice.*
> *The song became a big hit.*

A verb in this structure is called a linking verb, e.g. *be, become, get, look, seem.* The complement can be an adjective phrase (*nice*) or a noun phrase (*a big hit*).

D Subject + Verb + Adverbial
> *The match is tomorrow.*
> *We got on the bus.*
> *The meetings are every month.*

An adverbial can be an adverb phrase (*tomorrow*), a prepositional phrase (*on the bus*) or a noun phrase (*every month*).

E Subject + Verb + Object + Object
We should give the children presents.
Sarah sent me a text message.
Here there is a direct object (*a text message*) and an indirect object (*me*). ➤ 3

F Subject + Verb + Object + Complement
The project kept everyone very busy
All the publicity made the song a big hit.
Here the complement (*a big hit*) relates to the object of the clause (*the song*).

G Subject + Verb + Object + Adverbial
I put my mobile in my pocket.
The police got the car out of the river.
Here the adverbial (*out of the river*) relates to the object (*the car*).

H We can add extra adverbials to any of the clause structures.
*The visitors have **just** arrived.*
***To my surprise**, Sarah **actually** sent me a text message **right away**.*

TIP

With some verbs it is easy to predict the structure. *Give* usually has two objects; *put* always has an object + adverbial. But some verbs occur in different structures; for example *tell the truth* (one object) and *tell me a story* (two objects).

∽ *Give, send, buy*, etc

A Two objects

When a verb has two objects, the first is the indirect object, and the second is the direct object.

*You give **the attendant** your ticket.*
(NOT ~~You give your ticket the attendant.~~)
*We'll send **our teacher** a message.*
*Nigel bought **Celia** a diamond ring.*
*I can reserve **you** a seat.*

Here the indirect object (*you*) refers to the person receiving something, and the direct object (*a seat*) refers to the thing that is given.

B Object + prepositional phrase

Instead of an indirect object, we can use a prepositional phrase with *to* or *for*.

*You give your ticket **to** the attendant.*
*Nigel bought a diamond ring **for** Celia.*

The phrase with *to* or *for* comes after the direct object.

C *To* or *for*?

These verbs can go with *to*: award, fax, feed, give, grant, hand, leave (in a will), lend, mail, offer, owe, pass, pay, post, promise, read, sell, send, show, take, teach, tell, throw, write.

These verbs can go with *for*: buy, cook, fetch, find, fix, get, keep, leave, make, order, pick, reserve, save.

Bring goes with either *to* or *for*. You bring something *for* someone but *to* a place.

D Pronouns after *give*, *send*, etc

When there is a pronoun, it usually comes before a phrase with a noun.

*James lent **me** his mobile*
*I might send **them** to my sister.*

When there are two pronouns after the verb, we normally use *to* or *for*.

*We'll send **them to you** straight away.*
*My friend saved **it for me**.*

E *Describe, explain*, etc

Some verbs can occur with *to* or *for* but **not** with an indirect object.

Tim described the men to the police.
(NOT ~~Tim described the police the men.~~)
I'll explain everything to you.
(NOT ~~I'll explain you everything.~~)

Such verbs include *announce, communicate, deliver, describe, donate, explain, obtain, propose, purchase, report,* and *suggest.*

TIP

It is safer to use an indirect object only with a short verb like *give* or *send* and not with a longer verb like *describe* or *explain*.
Say *Can you give me the figures?*
but *Can you explain the figures to me?*

ᐱ **The use of statements**

A There are four sentence types. Each
has a main use.

- Statement (giving information)
  *You **took** a photo.*
- Question (asking for information)
  ***Did** you take a photo?*
- Imperative (an order or request)
  ***Take** a photo.*
- Exclamation (expressing a feeling)
  ***What** a nice photo!*

B Besides the main use, some sentence
types have other uses. For example, a
statement can ask for information.
  I want to hear all your latest news.
A question can be a request.
  Could you close the window, please?

C There are many uses (or
'communicative functions') of
statements, for example:

- Offering to do something
  I can carry that for you.
- Thanking someone
  I'm very grateful.
- Giving orders
  I'd like you to check these figures.

D Some present-simple verbs express
the use of the statement. They are
'performative verbs'. They include:

admit, advise, agree, apologize,
guarantee, insist, object, predict,
promise, protest, refuse, suggest, warn.

Here are some examples.
- Apologizing
  *It was my fault. I **apologize**.*
- Promising
  *I **promise** to behave myself.*
- Predicting
  *I **predict** a close game.*
- Suggesting
  *I **suggest** we all meet later.*

In general, performative verbs are
fairly emphatic, and some are rather
formal. For example, *I promise to*
behave is more emphatic than *I'll*
behave, and *I apologize* is more formal
than *I'm sorry.*

E Sometimes we use a modal verb before
a performative verb.
  *I'd **advise** you to shred the documents.*
  *I **must insist** we keep to the rules.*
  *I **can guarantee** you'll enjoy yourself.*

TIP

It is important to learn how statements
are used in communication. Some are
strongly associated with certain uses,
e.g. *I'm going to …* expresses an
intention, *I think you should …* gives
advice and *If only …* expresses a wish.

5 **Negative statements**

A In a negative statement, *not* or *n't* comes after the auxiliary verb. We write the auxiliary and *n't* together as one word.

> We **have not** received an invitation.
> The scheme **wasn't** working properly.

If there is more than one auxiliary, *not* or *n't* comes after the first auxiliary.

> We **shouldn't have** stayed so long.
> I **might not be** coming back next term.

B In simple tenses we use *do* as the auxiliary.

> I **don't** like cowboy films.
> The player **did not** speak to reporters.
> (NOT ~~The player spoke not to reporters.~~)

C *Be* on its own has *not* or *n't* after it.

> The area **is not/isn't** very nice.

D We do not use *no* in a negative verb form.

> The message **didn't** arrive.
> (NOT ~~The message no arrived.~~)

E *Not* can come before a word or phrase which needs correcting, or before some expressions of quantity, distance, or time.

> I ordered tea, **not coffee**.
> **Not many** people have their own aircraft.
> There's an internet café **not far** away.
> We arrived **not a moment** too soon.

F Other negative words

There are other words besides *not* which have a negative meaning.

	No, none, etc	*Not/n't*
no	We have **no** time.	We haven't **any** time.
none	Tickets? Oh, there are **none** left.	Tickets? Oh, there aren't **any** left.
no one, nobody	I saw **no one** acting strangely.	I didn't see **anyone** acting strangely.
nothing	I did **nothing** wrong.	I didn't do **anything** wrong.
nowhere	There was **nowhere** to park.	There wasn't **anywhere** to park.
few	**Few** people were interested.	**Not many** people were interested.
little	There was **little** interest.	There wasn't **much** interest.
never	I've **never** seen the film.	I haven't **ever** seen the film.
seldom, rarely	We **seldom** eat out.	We don't **often** eat out.
no longer	Adam **no longer** lives here.	Adam doesn't live here **any more**.
hardly, scarcely	I've **hardly** started on my project.	I haven't **really** started on my project.
neither, nor	You can't sing, and **neither** can I.	You can't sing, and I can't **either**.

11

○ Negatives with emphasis and inversion

A The emphatic negative

We can stress *not* or an auxiliary with *n't*.

I did **NOT** take your mobile.

I **DIDN'T** take your mobile.

We speak the word with extra force, and in writing we highlight the word, e.g. by underlining or using capital letters.

We can also use *at all* to emphasize a negative.

We don't like our new boss **at all**.

In no time **at all**, the tour was over.

At all usually goes at the end of a clause or after a negative phrase, e.g. *no time*.

Here are some other phrases which emphasize a negative.

The event did not go well **by any means**.

I'm not **in the least** hungry.

Her son's visits were **far from** frequent.

We can use *absolutely* before *no*, *nobody*, *nowhere*, etc.

There was **absolutely** nowhere to park.

We can use *whatever* or *whatsoever* after *nothing* or *none*, or after *no* + noun.

There's nothing **whatever** we can do about it.

I have no sympathy **whatsoever**.

B Inversion after a negative phrase

A negative phrase can come in front position. This can happen with phrases containing *no*, *never*, *neither*, *nor*, *seldom*, *rarely*, *hardly*, and *only*. The auxiliary (*should*) comes before the subject (*you*).

Under no circumstances should you travel alone.
(Compare: *You should not travel alone under any circumstances.*)
Never in my life have I seen such things.
The electricity had been disconnected – **nor** was there any water.
Only in summer is it hot enough to swim.

Sometimes a phrase with *not* can come in front position.

Not until the following Monday was I able to see a doctor.

If the verb is in a simple tense, we use the auxiliary verb *do*.

Seldom **do** we have any visitors.
(Compare: *We seldom have any visitors.*)
Only once **did** my attention wander.

TIP

A negative phrase with inversion can sound formal and literary. An exception is *no way*, which is informal, e.g. *No way can we get there on time.*

⌐ The imperative

A Form

The imperative is the base form of the verb, e.g. *wait, answer.*

Wait *a moment, please.*

Answer *all the questions.*

The negative is *do not/don't* + base form.

Do not remove *this book from the library.*

Don't make *so much fuss.*

For emphasis we use *do* + base form.

Do *be careful.*

B Use

The basic use of the imperative is to tell someone what to do. But this use is too abrupt in many situations, and there are more polite ways of telling people what to do. For more details, ➤ 8.

The imperative is also used in these contexts.

- Slogans and advertisements

  Save *the planet.* **Visit** *historic Bath.*

- Warnings and reminders

  Look *out! There's a car coming.*

  Don't forget *your key.*

- Instructions and directions

  Select *a document from the menu.*

  Turn *left at the lights.*

- Informal offers and invitations

  Have *a biscuit.* **Come** *to lunch.*

- Good wishes

  Have *a nice holiday.* **Enjoy** *yourselves.*

C Imperative + question tag

We can use a positive tag after a positive imperative.

*Come here, **will/would/can/could** you?*

The tag makes the imperative less abrupt.

Can't you? after an imperative expresses annoyance or impatience.

*Keep still, **can't you?***

In warnings and reminders, the tag is *won't you?* after a positive imperative and *will you?* after a negative.

*Drive carefully, **won't you?***
*Don't forget your key, **will you?***

D Let's

Let's + verb expresses a suggestion.

***Let's** go for a walk. ~ Good idea.*

The negative is *let's not* or (in British English) *don't let's*.

***Let's not** waste/**Don't let's** waste time.*

In British English we can use the tag *shall we?*

*Let's sit down, **shall we?***

TIP

You can use *Let me see* or *Let me think* to show that you are thinking about something, e.g. *Let me see. What else do we need?*

15

∞ Getting people to do things

A There are many different ways of
getting people to do things in English.
Compare these sentences.

I'd be very grateful if you could
translate this letter. (asking a favour)
Could you translate this letter, please?
(a polite request)
Translate this letter. (an instruction on
an exam paper)

The form we use for an order or
request depends on the situation.
It is usually necessary to use a polite
formula such as *Could you ...?* rather
than an imperative.

B To be very polite when asking a favour,
we need to use a longer formula.

Would you be so kind as to move into
the other room, please?
I wonder if you'd mind dealing with
the matter for me.

In most situations we use a question
form.

Could you sign here, please?
Would you mind giving me a lift?

It is always worth taking the trouble to
put your request into a question form.
It would not be polite to say simply
Give me a lift.

Even people in authority often use a
polite formula rather than an imperative.
> *Can you* get your books out, please?
> *I want you to* just keep still a moment.
> *You mustn't* spend too long on this.
> *I'd like you to* move closer together.
> *Would you like to* come this way?

C The imperative can be used to give orders.
> Teacher to pupils: *Open* your books, please.
> Doctor to patient: *Don't move*.
> Boss to employee: Now *print* out a copy.

But it is unusual to begin
a conversation with an imperative.
Often a polite formula is used first,
then a series of imperatives.
> *Can you* get out your books, please?
> *Open* them at page 60 and *look* at the
> photo. Then *think* about your reaction.

An imperative can also be used
informally between equals.
> *Give* me a hand with these boxes.
> *Hurry* up, or we're going to be late.

D This is how we ask to be given something.
> *Can/Could we have* our bill, please?
> *I'd like* an orange juice.
> A box of matches, *please*.

TIP

Rather than *Do it*, say *Could you do it,
please?* or *Would you mind doing it,
please?*

17

ᴓ Questions

A Types of question

There are two types: a yes/no question and a wh-question.

A yes/no question can be answered by *yes* or *no*.

> *Do you sell magazines?* ~ **Yes**, *we do.*
> *Will I need to pay?* ~ **No**, *it's free.*

The question begins with an auxiliary verb (*do, will*).

A wh-question begins with a question word.

> **When** *are you travelling?* ~ *Tomorrow.*
> **What** *should we do?* ~ *I don't know.*

For more details on question words,
➤ 10–11.

B Inversion in questions

In most questions there is inversion of the subject and auxiliary verb. (But ➤ 10C.)

> **Are you** *doing a course here?*
> *Why* **has the machine** *stopped?*
> *Where* **can we** *sit?*

Compare the statement **You are** *doing ...* and the question **Are you** *doing ...?*

If there is more than one auxiliary verb (e.g. *could* and *have*), then only the first one comes before the subject.

> **Could I have** *reserved a seat?*
> (NOT ~~Could have I reserved a seat?~~)

In simple tenses we use *do* as the
auxiliary.

> **Do** you like walking?
> Where **did** everyone stay?
> (NOT ~~Where stayed everyone?~~)

Be on its own as an ordinary verb also
comes before the subject.

> **Is this** cotton? Why **were you** late?
> (NOT ~~Why did you be late?~~)

C Questions without inversion

In informal conversation a question
can sometimes have the same word
order as a statement.

> **You were** late? ~ Yes, I'm afraid so.
> **They went** which way? ~ That way.

But this pattern is used less often in
English than in many other languages.

D Indirect questions

We can ask a question indirectly, and less
abruptly, by putting it into a sub-clause
with a question word or with *if/whether*.
There is no inversion in the sub-clause.

> Could you tell me **how much this costs**?
> I want to know **if I can book a seat**.

TIP

We use questions in many ways: not
only to ask for information, but also
to make requests (*Could you ...?*),
suggestions (*Shall we ...?*), offers (*Can
I ...?, Would you like to ...?*), and to ask
permission (*May I...?*).

10 Wh-questions

A Question words

These are the eight question words.

Who did Matt choose as his partner?
What are you reading?
Which is your car?
Whose is this newspaper?
Where do you work?
When did the accident happen?
Why is your friend so upset?
How did you manage to get a ticket?

B Question word + noun

What, *which*, and *whose* can have a noun (or adjective + noun) after them.

What action will you take?
Which day is best for you?
Whose stupid idea was this?

C Subject and object questions

When *who* or *what* is the subject of a question, there is no inversion. The word order is the same as in a statement. Compare these questions.

Subject: *Who invited you?* ~ Laura did.
(Someone invited you.)
Object: *Who did you invite?* ~ My friends.
(You invited someone.)

We can also use *how many* or *how much*.

How many people know the secret?
How much of the money was left?

Here are some more examples of a
question word as (part of) the subject.

Who *is organizing the trip?*
What *caused the accident?*
Which coat *suits me best?*
Whose car *was vandalized?*

D *Whom*

In formal English, when *who* is the object,
we can use *whom* instead. (See Tip.)

Who/Whom *did you invite?*

E Prepositions in questions

A question word can be the object of a
preposition.

Where *is Maria **from**?*
(She is **from somewhere**.)
What *are you looking **at**?*
(You are looking **at something**.)

Usually the preposition comes in
the same place as in a statement
(*looking **at***). But in formal English
the preposition can come before the
question word.

To which *hospital was the boy taken?*

Note the patterns with *who/whom*.

Who *were you talking **to**?*
To whom *were you talking?* (formal)

TIP

Whom is formal and old-fashioned.
Say *Who do you know?* not *Whom do
you know?*

11 More on question words

A *Who, what,* and *which*

Who always refers to a human.
> **Who** is your tutor?

We cannot use *who* before a noun or *of.*
> NOT ~~Who tutor ...?~~
> NOT ~~Who of the tutors ...?~~

Which can refer to a human or to something non-human.
> **Which** tutor do you have?
> **Which** printer/**Which** of these printers is cheapest?

What refers to something non-human, but *what* + noun can refer to a human.
> **What** (programme) did you watch?
> **What** idiot broke this?

What implies an indefinite (and often large) number of possible answers.
> **What** sport do you play?

Which implies a definite (and often small) number of answers.
> **Which** way is it, right or left?

In some contexts either word is possible.
> **What/Which** size shoe do you take?
> **What/Which** languages can you speak?

B Question phrases

What can combine with other words, mainly nouns.
> **What time** is the next train?
> **What about** some lunch? ~ Good idea.

Note also *what colour*, *what make*,
what kind/type/sort of and *what ...
like?*

What's your teacher **like**? ~ She's nice.

How can also combine with other
words, mainly adjectives and adverbs.

How old is this building?

How far did you walk?

Note also *how often*, *how long*, *how
many*, and *how much*.

How many people live in the building?

C Modifying a question word

We can ask for exact information with
exactly or *precisely*.

When are you leaving **exactly**?

What **precisely** does the job involve?

We can ask for approximate
information with *roughly*,
approximately, and, before a question
phrase, *about*.

Roughly how many customers do you
get in a day?

Approximately how far is it?

About what time will we arrive?

TIP

We can emphasize a wh-question with
on earth or with *ever*, e.g. *Where on
earth have you been? Whatever / What
ever can the matter be?*

---

12 Negative questions

A A negative yes/no question often
expresses surprise.

> **Aren't** you ready yet?
> (I am surprised that you are not
> ready.)

A negative yes/no question or
a question with *why* can be a
complaint.

> **Can't** you turn the volume down?
> **Why hasn't** the job been done?

We can use *Why don't we/you...?* or
Why not + verb ...? for a suggestion.

> **Why don't** you take a taxi?
> **Why not** use your credit card?

B Negative questions with *who, what,* or
which usually ask for information.

> **Who hasn't** returned this library book?
> **What can't** you understand?
> **Which** computer **isn't** working?

C We can use a negative yes/no question
to ask the hearer to agree.

> **Isn't** there a quicker way?
> **Haven't** we met somewhere before?
> The meaning is similar to *We've met*
> *somewhere before, haven't we?*

D We make a question negative by putting *n't* after the auxiliary.
Positive: ***Do** you like chocolate?*
Negative: ***Don't** you like chocolate?*

The negative of *am I* is *aren't I*.
*Why **aren't I** on the list?*

We do not use *not* after the auxiliary.
NOT *Do not you like chocolate?*
But in more formal English *not* can come after the subject.
*Are we **not** a democratic people?*

We can use other negative words. ➤ 5F
*Are you **never** going to finish?*
*Is there **no** electricity?*

E If a question word is the subject, *n't* or *not* comes after the auxiliary.
Positive: *Who **has** got a ticket?*
Negative: *Who **hasn't/has not** got a ticket?*

We can also use other negative words in a wh-question.
Positive: *Have you **ever** been skiing?*
Negative: *Have you **never** been skiing?*

TIP

Be careful when answering a yes/no negative question. *No* agrees that the negative is true. *Yes* means that the positive is true. For example, *Aren't you ready? ~ No, but I will be in ten minutes./Yes, I am. Let's go.*

25

13 Answering questions

A Some questions can be answered in a word or phrase, but others need a longer answer.

*What colour is your car? ~ **Blue**.*
*When is your exam? ~ **Next Thursday**.*
*How is Lucy? ~ **Oh, a lot better, thank you. She'll be back at work next week**.*

It is usually enough to give the relevant information. You do not need to say *My car is blue* in the first answer.

B We can sometimes answer with just *yes* or *no*, but a **short answer** is often better.

***Is it** raining? ~ Yes, **it is**.*
***Can Alice** swim? ~ No, **she can't**.*

A short answer relates to the subject and auxiliary verb of the question (*your sister* and *can*). A positive answer is: *yes* + pronoun + auxiliary. A negative answer is: *no* + pronoun + auxiliary + *n't*.

In simple tenses we use the auxiliary *do*.

***Do you** like it? ~ Yes, **I do**.*
***Did we** succeed? ~ No, we **didn't**.*

We can use *be* as an ordinary verb.

***Are you** late? ~ Yes, **I am**./No, **I'm not**.*

C We can sometimes use another phrase or clause instead of *yes* or *no*.

*Am I the winner? ~ **Of course** you are.*
*Did you fail? ~ **I'm afraid** I did.*

We often add information or a comment after a simple *yes* or *no*, or after a short answer.

*Were you late? ~ Yes, **I missed the bus**.*

*Did Carl get the job he wanted? ~ No, he didn't, **unfortunately**.*

*Have you seen the film? ~ Yes, I have. **I really enjoyed it**.*

D We cannot normally use a short answer to reply to a request, offer, invitation, or suggestion.

*Can I use your phone? ~ **Of course**.*

*Would you like a sweet? ~ **Yes, please**.*

*Would you like to come to my party? ~ **Yes, I'd love to**. **Thank you very much**.*

*Shall we have a coffee? ~ **Good idea**.*

We cannot answer *Yes, we shall*.

A negative answer to a request, invitation, or suggestion needs some explanation.

*Can I use your phone? ~ **Sorry, someone's using it at the moment**.*

*Would you like to come to my party? ~ **I'd love to, but I'll be away this weekend**.*

TIP

In some situations it can seem unhelpful to simply answer *Yes* or *Yes, it is*. In a friendly conversation, try to add something to keep the conversation going, e.g. *Is that watch new? ~ Yes, it is. I bought it last week.*

14 Question tags

A Form

A question tag refers back to the subject and auxiliary of the main clause.

Subject	Aux.		Tag
Paul	*was*	*joking,*	**wasn't he?**

A negative tag is auxiliary + *n't* + pronoun (*wasn't he?*).

A positive tag is like a negative one, but without *n't*.

*Paul wasn't joking, **was he?***

In simple tenses we use the auxiliary *do*.

*You came home early, **didn't you?***

We can use *be* as an ordinary verb.

*That wasn't very clever, **was it?***

After *I am*, the tag is *aren't I?*

*I'm late, **aren't I?***

B More about pronouns

We can use the subject *there* in a tag.

*There's lots to do, isn't **there?***

After *this/that* or *-thing*, we use *it*.

*That's right, isn't **it?*** (NOT *... isn't that?*)
*Something went wrong, didn't **it?***

After *these/those* or *-one/-body*, we use *they*.

*These CDs are cheap, aren't **they?***
*Anybody could just walk in, couldn't **they?***

C Positive and negative

The usual patterns are these:

- positive statement + negative tag
- negative statement + positive tag.

These tags ask the hearer to agree that the statement is true. It is usually an invitation to continue the conversation.

*It's cold, **isn't it?***
*It isn't very warm, **is it?***

The intonation falls on the tag because the statement is clearly true. But the voice can rise when the sentence is like a question.

*You've got the tickets, **haven't you?***

We can use this rising intonation in a question or request.

*You couldn't lend me £10, **could you?***

D Positive statement + positive tag

This pattern has a different meaning from the examples above.

I've got no time at the moment. ~
*You're busy, **are you?***
*Vicky doesn't live here any more. ~ Oh, she's moved, **has she?***

This means that I realize from what you say that she has moved, and I want you to confirm this and continue the conversation.

TIP

Tags are useful when you are making friendly remarks, e.g. about the weather.

29

15 Echo questions, echo tags, and exclamations

A Echo questions

We can use an echo question when we do not understand something or we find it hard to believe. The voice rises on the question word.

I often eat bits of wood. ~ **What** *do you eat? / You eat* **what?**

My father knew Oprah Winfrey. ~ **Who** *did he know? / He knew* **who?**

Did you see the naked lady? ~ *Did I see the* **what?**

B Echo tags

We form an echo tag like a question tag (➤ 14). A positive statement has a positive tag, and a negative statement has a negative tag.

I'm leaving my job. ~ *Oh,* **are you?**
The printer doesn't work. ~ **Doesn't it?** *Oh, dear.*

An echo tag expresses interest.

Now look at these examples.

I'm leaving my job. ~ *You aren't,* **are you?**

The printer doesn't work. ~ *It does,* **doesn't it?** *I've just been using it.*

Max won the prize. ~ *He didn't,* **did he?**

This expresses surprise or disbelief. I didn't expect Max to win the prize.

We can use a negative tag to reply to a positive statement.

*The music was great. ~ Yes, **wasn't it**?*

We both agree that the music was great.

C Exclamations

An exclamation is any phrase or sentence spoken with emphasis and feeling.

Oh no!   Lovely!   You idiot!   Stop!

There are patterns with *how* and *what* that can be used in an exclamation, although not always with an exclamation mark (!).

After *how* we can use an adjective, an adverb, or a subject + verb.

***How** awful!   **How** nice to see you.*

*Look at the plants – **how** they've grown!*

After *what* there can be a noun phrase with *a/an* or without an article.

***What** a surprise!   **What** a good idea.*

***What** nonsense you talk.*

Some exclamations have the form of a negative question.

***Aren't** you lucky.   **Don't** you look smart!*

(This means that you look very smart.)

TIP

You can use an echo tag to agree with a friendly statement, e.g. *Lovely day! ~ Beautiful, isn't it?*

---

16 Replacing and leaving out words

A We often avoid repeating a word when it is not necessary to do so. For example, we replace a noun phrase with a pronoun.
*Where's Kirsty? **She**'s late.*

B We can also leave out a noun after a number, a quantifier, *this/that/these/those*, or a superlative adjective.
*Have you got a sister? ~ I've got **two**.*
*There's soup here. Would you like **some**?*
(NOT *Would you like?*)
*These shirts are cotton, but **those** aren't.*
*Which question was the **most difficult**?*

C To avoid repeating a to-infinitive, we can often leave out the words after *to*.
*Would you like to join us? ~ I'd love **to**.*
*I got the job, although I didn't expect **to**.*
But we repeat an auxiliary after *to*.
*I was chosen for the job, although I didn't expect to **be**.*

After *like*, *try*, and *want*, we often leave out *to* as well.
*You can stay as long as you **like**.*

D The main verb can sometimes be left out.
Arsenal have won six games and Chelsea five. (= ... and Chelsea **have won** five.)

E In conversational English certain kinds of words can be left off the beginning of a sentence if the meaning is still clear.

Can't find my keys. (= **I** can't find ...)
Sorry about that. (= **I'm** sorry ...)
Getting dark now. (= **It's** getting ...)
Everything OK? (**Is** everything OK?)
Tired? (**Are you** tired?)

F In some special styles of English, words are left out to save space. This happens in newspaper headlines and in instructions.

Six arrested in raid. (Six **people have been** arrested in **a** raid.)
Insert battery. (Insert **the** battery.)

Note style is used when it is necessary to be brief, e.g. when writing a postcard.

Hotel fine, weather marvellous. (**The** hotel **is** fine, **and the** weather **is** marvellous.)

Text messages often use note style and abbreviations.

Arrive 30 mins. CU soon.

TIP

It is not always possible to avoid repetition. Look at this sentence: *I bought some sweets and biscuits, but I've eaten all the sweets.* We need to repeat *sweets* here to make the meaning clear.

17 Leaving out words after the auxiliary

A A clause can end with an auxiliary if the meaning is clear from the context.

*I haven't brought a map, but Laura **has**.*
*The meeting went on longer than I thought it **would**.*

In simple tenses we use *do*.
*Don't leave. You'll be sorry if you **do**.*
We also use the ordinary verb *be*.
*This sweater isn't dry. ~ This one **is**.*

B The auxiliary can be positive or negative. A positive auxiliary cannot be a short form.

*Am I too late? ~ I'm afraid you **are**.*
(NOT *I'm afraid you're.*)
But the negative can be *n't*.
*Of course you **aren't**.*

C In some contexts we put a tag or an adverbial after the auxiliary.

*That's a nice colour. ~ It is, **isn't it**?*
*Is there a market today? ~ I don't know. There was **yesterday**.*

D Sometimes we have to use two auxiliary verbs. When both are in the previous clause, we can leave out the second.

*You could have hurt yourself. ~ Yes, I suppose I **could** (**have**).*

When the first auxiliary is new in the context, we cannot leave out the second.
*Have the team won? ~ They look happy, so they **must have**.*
*Is Tom still waiting? ~ He **might be**.*
*When will the grass be cut? ~ It already **has been**.*

E A short yes/no question consists of an auxiliary + subject.
*I've never been to New York. **Have you**?*
*I wanted Karen to do well in her exam. ~ And **did she**? ~ Yes, she did very well.*

In a short wh-question, we simply use a question word or question phrase.
*I'm giving up my course. ~ Oh, **why**?*
*I've got a meeting today. ~ **What time**?*
When the question word is the subject, the auxiliary can come after it.
*Something's happened. ~ What (**has**)?*

A sub-clause can also end with a question word if the meaning is clear.
*The road is closed. No one knows **why**.*
*I put the card somewhere, but I can't remember **where**.*

TIP

You can end a clause with a negative auxiliary when contradicting someone:
What time did you have breakfast? ~ I didn't. I never have breakfast.

---

18 *Too, either, so,* and *neither/ nor*

A *Too* and *either*

After a clause there can be a short addition with *too* or *either*, to say that what is true of one thing is also true of another.

Positive:
subject + auxiliary + *too*
> *I'm falling asleep.* ~ ***I am, too.***
> *I've spent all my money.* ~ ***I have too.***

Negative:
subject + auxiliary + *n't* + *either*
> *I haven't got a watch.* ~ ***I haven't, either.***
> *Tom can't drive, and **Emma can't either.***

In simple tenses we use *do.*
> *This pen doesn't work. And **this one doesn't either.***
> *I enjoyed the film.* ~ ***I did, too.***

We can also use *be* as an ordinary verb.
> *I'm not hungry.* ~ ***I'm not either.***

B *So* and *neither/nor*

We can also form a short addition with *so* and *neither/nor.* Here *so* means 'too' or 'also'.

Positive:
so + auxiliary + subject
> *I'm falling asleep.* ~ ***So am I.***
> *You're beautiful.* ~ ***So are you.***

Negative:
neither/nor + auxiliary + subject
 *I'm not going. ~ **Nor am I**.*
 *Tom can't drive, and **neither can***
 ***Emma**.*
So am I means the same as I am, too
and *Nor am I means the same as I'm*
not either.

C Negative after positive; positive after negative

In these examples, a negative addition
follows a positive statement, and a
positive addition follows a negative
statement. Something which is true of
one thing is not true of another.
 *I'm tired, ~ Well, **I'm not**.*
 *We didn't enjoy the film. ~ Oh, **we did**.*
The stress is on *I* and *we*.

We can also use a short statement to
contradict what someone says.
 *You're tired. ~ No, **I'm not**.*
 *I can't sing. ~ **You can**, you know*
The stress here is on *not* in the first
and on *can* in the second.

TIP

In informal English you can use *Me too*
or *Me neither* for a short addition about
yourself, e.g. *I'd love to go to India. ~
Me too. I haven't had a holiday this
year. ~ Me neither.*

19 *Think so, hope not,* etc

A *So* replacing a clause

So can replace a whole clause.

*Will you be going out? ~ Yes, I expect **so**.*
(= I expect **I will be going out**.)
*Are these figures correct? ~ I think **so**.*

We cannot leave out *so* or use *it*.

NOT *Yes, I expect.* OR *Yes, I expect it.*

With *so* we can use: *be afraid, it appears/appeared, assume, believe, expect, guess, hope, imagine, presume, say, it seems/seemed, suppose, suspect, tell (someone), think.*

B *So* or *not* in the negative

There are two negative patterns:

* negative verb + *so*
  *Will you be late in? ~ I **don't** expect **so**.*
* positive verb + *not*
  *Is it going to rain? ~ I hope **not**.*

With *expect, imagine,* and *think,* we usually form the negative with *so*.

*Is the boss in? ~ I **don't** think **so**.*
I think not is possible but rather formal.

Some verbs and expressions always form the negative with *not*.

*There's no point in waiting. ~ I guess **not**.*
(NOT *I don't guess so.*)

In this pattern we use *be afraid, assume, guess, hope, presume,* and *suspect*.

We can use these verbs in either pattern:
appear, believe, say, seem, suppose.
We aren't going to win a prize. ~ No, I
*don't suppose **so**. / No, I suppose **not**.*

C *So* at the beginning

With *appear, assume, believe, say,*
seem, and *understand,* we can use *so* at
the beginning of a clause to comment
on the truth of a statement.
*Will there be a party? ~ **So I've heard**.*
*Are the tickets all sold? ~ **So they say**.*
*Our tutor had a late night. ~ **So it seems**.*

D *If so* and *if not*

So and *not* can replace a clause after *if.*
*Need a loan? **If so**, give us a ring.*
(If you need a loan, ...)
*Have you got transport? **If not**, I can*
give you a lift.
(If you haven't got transport, ...)

E *Not* after an adverb

We can use *not* after certain adverbs,
e.g. *certainly, definitely, maybe, of*
course, perhaps, possibly, probably.
Are you going to accept the offer? ~
*No, **certainly not**.*

TIP

Do not use *so* with *know* and *sure*. Say
Yes, I know and *Are you sure?*

---

20 More patterns with *so*

A *Do so, do it,* and *do that*

We can use *do so* or *do it* to avoid
repeating an action verb and the words
after it. *Do so* is a little formal.
> *If you haven't paid yet, please **do so** now.*
> *She had always wanted to fly a plane,*
> *and now at last she was **doing so/it**.*

The stress is on *do*.

With *do that,* we usually stress *that*.
> *The plates need washing. ~ I'll **do that**.*
> *I'd like to burn that building down. ~*
> *I wouldn't **do that** if I were you.*

In the last example we stress *that* to
express surprise or shock at the action.

B *So* in short answers

A short answer with *so* can express
agreement. The pattern is *so* +
pronoun + auxiliary or *be*.
> *This is a one-way street. ~ Oh, **so it is**.*

The speaker is noticing or
remembering that it is a one-way street.

Compare these two patterns.
> *You've made a mistake. ~ **So I have**.*
> (= I agree I have made a mistake.)
> *I've made a mistake. ~ **So have I**.*
> (= I have made a mistake, too.)

C *So* and *that way*

In formal English *so* can replace an adjective after *become* and *remain*.

The situation is not yet serious, but it may become so. (= become **serious**)

Get/stay that way is more informal.

*The situation isn't serious yet, but it may get **that way**.*

We can also use *so* after *more* or *less*.
*It's often busy here – more **so** in summer.*

D *The same*

The same can replace words just mentioned, e.g. an object or complement.

*I'm having steak. ~ I'll have **the same**.*

*Monday was pretty hot, and Tuesday was **the same**.*

We can use *do/say/think the same (thing), feel the same (way)*, and *The same is true of ... / The same goes for ....*

*One night Alan walked in his sleep. Next night he **did the same thing**.*

*The others think we should stay together, and I **think the same**.*

*Rents are very high here, but **the same goes for** lots of other towns.*

TIP

When someone wishes you a happy new year or a nice weekend, you can return the good wishes by answering *The same to you.*

21 Word order and information

A Imagine you are sitting in a café with a friend drinking a cup of coffee when one of you makes this comment.

This coffee tastes awful.

This statement begins with the subject (*This coffee*) and the verb (*tastes*), the normal word order in a statement. Here a complement (*awful*) follows the verb.

We can also look at the sentence from the point of view of the information it communicates. The first phrase (*This coffee*) is the **topic**, what the sentence is about. The last phrase (*awful*) is the important **information** about the topic. *This coffee* is 'old information' because it is naturally in our thoughts in the situation. *Awful* is 'new information', the point of the message. The sentence starts with old information and then tells us something new about it. This is a typical way of communicating information, although it is certainly not an absolute rule.

B A sentence in a text also typically starts with old information, something mentioned in the previous sentence.

*Health workers want big pay rises. **The nurses** may even go on strike.*
*There was a huge explosion. **It** was heard ten miles away.*

In each of the last two examples, the second sentence links to the previous one by mentioning old information (*health workers* ← *nurses*) or using a pronoun (*explosion* ← *it*).

A clause or sentence can also begin by making a contrast with something in the previous one.

> Fifty years ago, not many people flew, but **today** air travel is much more common.

C Compare these two sentences.

> The girls did well. **Amy** won first prize.
> There were lots of prizes. **First prize** went to Amy.

We choose a structure which links the subject to the previous sentence.

D Sometimes we can use an abstract noun referring back to an idea.

> Someone threw a stone through the window. **This incident** upset everyone.
> The people here have nothing. **Their poverty** is extreme.

TIP

When writing a connected text such as an email or a letter, try to link sentences by starting with known information and saying something new about it.

---

22 Phrases in front position

The subject often comes in front
position (at the beginning of a sentence).
But sometimes we put another phrase
before the subject. We do this to make
the phrase more prominent.

A Adverbial in front position

Most kinds of adverbial can go in front
position. ➤ 121A

   Adam hasn't come. ***Maybe*** *he's forgotten.*
   I didn't lock the car. ***Luckily*** *it's still there.*

Adverbials of time often go in front
position to help show the sequence of
events.

   First *you mix the sand and cement, and*
   then *you add water.*

An adverb of manner in front position
is rather literary.

   Slowly *the sun sank into the Pacific.*

B Inversion after an adverbial

When an adverbial of place comes
in front position, there is sometimes
inversion of subject and verb.

   Daniel walked along to number 16.
   Outside the house *was a large van.*
   There was just a table and two chairs in
   the room. ***On the table*** *lay a newspaper.*

Inversion happens with verbs of place and movement, e.g. *be, come, go, lie, sit, stand.* There is no inversion with other verbs.

*Outside two men **were talking**.*
(NOT ~~Outside were talking two men.~~)

C Inversion after *here/there*

We can use *here* and *there* in front position to draw attention to something. There is inversion of subject and verb.

***Here** is an announcement.*
***There** goes the bus, look.*

In this pattern we can use *be, come,* or *go* in the present simple.

· When the subject is a pronoun, there is no inversion.

*Where's my bag? ~ Here **it is**.*
*The kids are back. Here **they come**.*

D Object and complement

We can put an object or complement in front position for emphasis when it links or contrasts with what has gone before.

*Do you prefer cats or dogs? ~ **Dogs** I love, but **cats** I can't stand.*
*The scheme has many good points. **One advantage** is the low cost.*

TIP

There are no fixed rules about what goes in front position. You can also say *I love dogs, but I can't stand cats.* It is a matter of style and emphasis.

23 The empty subject *there*

A To point out the existence of something, we use *there* + *be*.
  There's *hot water in the kettle.*
  There are *some letters for you.*
  There was *an accident here last week.*
  There were *ten people in the queue.*
  There must have been *a power cut.*
The verb *be* agrees with the noun phrase after it: *There* **is/was** *a letter,* but *There* **are/were** *some letters.* But in informal speech you may hear *there's* before a plural: *There's some letters.*

For the choice of *there* and *it,* ➤ 24D.

B We form negatives and questions with *there* in the normal way.
  There isn't *any hot water.*
  Are there *any letters for me?*
  What is there *to do in this place?*
We often use *no* with a noun.
  There's **no** *hot water.*

We can use *there* in a question tag.
  There's enough time, **isn't there?**

C *There* can be the subject of a to-infinitive or an ing-form, although this is rather literary.
  I didn't expect **there to be** *such a crowd.*
  I love the idea of **there being** *life forms elsewhere in the universe.*

D We can use this pattern with *there* and
an active or a passive participle.
> **There's** someone **waiting** for you.
> (= Someone is waiting for you.)
> **There was** a van **parked** by the house.
> (= A van was parked by the house.)

But we do not use a participle for a
single complete action.
> **There was** a noise **that woke** me up.
> (NOT <s>There was a noise waking me up.</s>)

When the relative pronoun is not the
subject, we cannot use a participle.
> **There's** something **that I need** to do.
> (NOT <s>There's something needing to do.</s>)

E After *there*, other verbs are possible,
but only in a formal or literary style.
> Nearby **there stands** an ancient tower.
> **There** now **follows** a short interval.

These verbs include: *appear, arise, arrive,
come, enter, exist, follow, lie, live, occur,
remain, result, sit, stand, take place*.

Between *there* and *be* we can use
*appear, chance, happen, prove, seem,
tend, turn out*, or *use*.
> **There seems to be** no truth in the story.

TIP

To mention that something exists, say,
e.g. *There's a bus service*, not <s>A bus service is</s>.

---

24 The empty subject *it*

A We can use *it* to refer to the time, distance, the environment, or the weather.

It's half past three.
How far is it to the hotel?
It'll be busy in town.
It was cold yesterday.

B Each of these sentences has a clause as its subject.

***To make new friends** is difficult.*
***That it rained** was a pity.*

This word order is possible but not very usual. Instead we use the subject *it*, and the clause comes later in the sentence.

It's difficult to make new friends.
It was a pity that it rained.
It amazes me how much things cost.

With a gerund clause we use both patterns.

***Making new friends** is difficult.*
It's difficult making new friends.

We can also use *it* in the pattern: subject + verb + *it* + complement + clause.

I find it difficult to make new friends.
We all thought it a pity that it rained.
(NOT ~~We all thought that it rained a pity.~~)

C *It* can also be an empty subject before *appear, happen, seem,* and *turn out*.

It seems the phone is out of order.
It turned out that the card was stolen.

Note also the patterns *it looks as if / as though* and *it seems as if / as though*.
> **It looks as if** it's going to rain.
> **It seems as though** we're not welcome.

D *It* and *there* can both be empty subjects, but they are used in different ways. *There + be* expresses the fact that something exists or happens. *It + be* refers to something definite and known in the situation, or it refers to the time or the environment.
> **There's** someone at the door. **It's** Jade.
> **It** was Saturday, so **there** weren't any classes.
> **There's** quite a wind today. ~ Yes, **it's** really windy, isn't it?

We normally use *there* with a noun phrase of indefinite meaning, e.g. **someone**, **any** classes, **a** wind.

Compare these patterns.
> **There** isn't any truth in the story.
> The story **has** no truth in it.

And compare this pattern with *it* referring forward to a clause.
> **It** isn't true what they say.

TIP

Don't start a sentence with a clause, especially in speech. Say *It was lovely to see you again*, not ~~To see you again was lovely~~.

49

25 Emphasis

A Emphatic stress

We can speak a word with greater force to make it more prominent and often to contrast it with something else.

> I wanted a **large** packet, not a small one.

In writing we can use CAPITAL LETTERS, *italics*, **bold** or <u>underlining</u>.

We can stress a word expressing an extreme quality or feeling.

> It's a **huge** building.
> I'd **love** a cup of coffee.
> I've got a **terrible** memory.

When a word has two or more syllables, only one syllable is spoken with stress. *Terr* has extra stress, but *ible* is weakly stressed.

B Emphasis in the verb phrase

We can stress the auxiliary or the ordinary verb *be*.

> Yes, I **can** swim – quite well, in fact.
> I **wasn't** asleep. I was listening.

We say *Yes, I* CAN *swim* in order to emphasize the positive meaning.

In a simple tense we use *do*.

> Oh, your garden **does** look nice.
> I'm quite sure I **did** download the file.

We do not need to mark emphatic *do* in writing: *Your garden does look nice.*

Look at these examples.
*We **might** go away for the weekend.*
(possibly, not definitely)
*I **did** have an MP3 player once.*
(in the past, not now)

C Emphasis with *it*

To emphasize a phrase, we can use
it + *be* + phrase + relative clause.
Didn't Edison invent the telephone? ~
*No, **it was Bell** who invented the phone.*
***It's the light bulb** that Edison invented.*
***It was me** who suggested the idea.*
***It's today**, not tomorrow, that we leave.*

D Emphasis with *what*

We can use a what-clause + *be* to
emphasize part of a sentence.
***What** caused the crash **was bad driving**.*
***What** you need **is a holiday**.*
***What** I long for **is a little excitement**.*
***What** we did **was (to) leave at once**.*

We cannot use *who* in this pattern. We
use *The person/people who ...*
***The people who** caused all the trouble
are friends of Hannah's.*
(NOT *Who caused all the trouble are ...*)

TIP

Many people think it is impolite to use
CAPITALS in an e-mail. You can use asterisks
for emphasis, e.g. *It is *essential* that you
attend the meeting.*

26 The present simple

Form

A The present simple is the base form of a verb, e.g. *know, take*.

You **know** the answer.

I usually **take** the bus.

The third person singular has *-s* or *-es*.

Tom **knows** the answer.

This colour **matches** my jacket.

For pronunciation, spelling, and other details of the s-form, ➤ 177A.

B In the negative we use *do not* or *don't* + base form.

I just **do not know** the answer.

The instructions **don't make** sense.

In the third person singular we use *does not* or *doesn't* + base form.

Tom **does not know** the answer.

The journey **doesn't take** long.

(NOT ... ~~no takes long.~~ AND NOT ... ~~doesn't takes long.~~)

C In questions we use *do* + base form.

Do you **know** the answer?

What **do** the instructions **say**?

In the third person singular we use *does*.

Does Tom **know** the answer?

How long **does** the journey **take**?

(NOT ~~How long takes the journey?~~)

We do not use *do* with *be* (➤ 44C) but we sometimes use it with *have* (➤ 45F).

Basic uses

D We use the present simple for a present state (➤ 36), e.g. a feeling, an opinion, or the fact that something belongs to someone.

*My girlfriend **likes** hiphop.*
*Do you **think** it's a good idea?*
*This MP3 player **belongs** to my brother.*

We also use the present simple for facts such as what or where things are.

*Silicon **is** a chemical element.*
*York **lies** on the River Ouse.*

E We also use the present simple for repeated actions such as routines, habits, jobs, hobbies, and things that always happen.

*The old man **walks** his dogs every day.*
*I **work** in Oxford. I usually **drive** to work.*
*We **play** volleyball on Wednesdays.*
*I **don't see** my cousins very often.*

Typical time expressions with the present simple are *always, often, usually, sometimes, ever/never; every day/week,* etc; *once/twice a week,* etc; *on Friday(s),* etc; *in the morning(s)/ evening(s), at ten o'clock,* etc.

TIP

Use the present simple to make generalizations, e.g. *The British don't like living in flats,* and to make scientific statements, e.g. *Food gives you energy.*

27 The present continuous

Form

A The present continuous is the present
of *be* + ing-form. ✓

> *I'm writing an email.*
> *Those people are waiting for a taxi.*
> *It's raining now, look.*

For spelling of the ing-form, ➤ 178.

B In the negative we use *not* or *n't* after
be.

> *I'm not making a noise.*
> *They aren't playing / They're not
> playing very well.*
> *It isn't raining. / It's not raining.*

C In questions we put *be* before the
subject.

> *Am I doing it right?*
> *Is it still raining?*
> *Where are you calling from?*

Use

D We use the present continuous for a
present action over a period of time,
something that we are in the middle
of now. The action has started, but it
hasn't finished yet.

> *Someone is following us.*
> *What are you doing?* ~ *I'm thinking.*
> *It's a lovely day, and we're all sitting in
> the garden.*

Some typical time expressions with the present continuous are *now*, *at the moment*, *at present*, *just*, *already*, and *still*.

The train is leaving Victoria **now**.
We're having tea **at the moment**.
I won't be long. I'm **just** ironing this shirt.
The customer is **still** waiting to be served.

The action does not need to be going on at the moment of speaking.

I**'m reading** an interesting book at the moment.
(I do not have the book in my hands.)
Is anyone **sitting** here? ~ No, it's free.
(asking permission to take a seat)

The important thing is that the action has started but not finished.

E We also use the present continuous for a temporary routine, something that will last only a short time.

We've got builders at the office, so I**'m working** at home this week.
They**'re living** in a rented flat until they find somewhere to buy.

Typical time expressions are *this week*, *these days*, *nowadays*, *at/for the moment*, *at present*, and *still*.

TIP

We use the present continuous to talk about things that are developing or changing over a long period, e.g. *The earth is getting warmer*.

28 Present simple or present continuous?

A The basic difference

We use the present simple for a permanent routine, a state, or a fact.

*We **eat** in the canteen most days.*
*Paul **loves** burgers.*
*Two and two **makes** four.*

We use the present continuous for something we are in the middle of.

*I'm **eating** a burger at the moment.*

These forms can refer to the future, ➤ 40.

B Routines

We use the simple for a permanent routine and the continuous for a temporary routine.

*I usually **travel** to work by car, but it's off the road. I'm **travelling** by bus this week.*

C *Always*

Always with the continuous means 'very often'. It sometimes expresses annoyance.

*I'm **always losing** things.*

Compare these sentences.

*We **always have** a test.* (every lesson)
*We're **always having** tests.* (very often)

D States

We use the present simple for a state.

➤ 36A

*We **need** more money.*

Some verbs can be either simple or continuous. For more details, ➤ 36B, 36D.

*The weather **looks/is looking** nice.*

E Present actions

The present simple can be used to describe actions as they happen.

*He **shoots**! And it's a goal!*
*I **add** the sauce and **stir** gently.*

For *I agree, I apologize*, etc ➤ 4D.

F Past actions

We can use the present tense for past events to make a story come to life.

*I**'m standing** there, and a man **comes** up to me and **grabs** me by the arm ...*

We can also use the present to explain the plot of a story.

*Macbeth **murders** the King of Scotland, who **is staying** at his castle.*

G The written word

We use the present simple to report the written word.

*It **says** in the paper the game is today.*
*The letter **explains** everything.*

We can also use it for what someone has said recently.

*Laura **says** she doesn't feel well.*

> **TIP**
>
> Use the present simple in instructions and explanations, e.g. *You pull down the File menu and choose Print.*

29 The past simple

Form

A With most verbs we add -*ed* to form the past simple

> We **finished** our meal and **walked** home.
> They **played** football on Tuesday.

The form is the same in all persons. For pronunciation and spelling, ➤ 177B, 178B.

Some past forms are irregular.

> When they **saw** the fire, they **ran** away.

For a list of irregular verbs, ➤ page 362.

B In the negative we use *did not* or *didn't* + base form.

> We **didn't finish** our meal.
> They **didn't run** away.
> (NOT *They no ran away.*
> AND NOT *They didn't ran away.*)

In questions we use *did* + base form.

> **Did** they **finish** their meal?
> How fast **did** they **run**?
> (NOT *How fast ran they?*)

C Both regular and irregular verbs are the same in all persons. The one exception is the verb *be*. ➤ 44C

> I **was** / You **were** late this morning.

We do not use *did* with *was* or *were*.
*I **wasn't** hungry at lunch.*
***Were** you tired last night?*
(NOT ~~Did you be tired last night?~~)

Use

D We use the past simple for an action in the past.
*I **bought** this coat yesterday.*
*I **saw** the film three weeks ago.*
*The war **ended** in 1945.*
*When **did** the train **arrive**?*
The time of the action (*yesterday, three weeks ago*) is over.

The past is the normal tense in stories.
*A princess once **walked** into a wood and **sat** down by a stream ...*

E The past simple can also refer to a series of actions in the past.
*I often **visited** this place as a child.*
*He **went** to the Job Centre several times.*

We also use the past simple for states.
*That party last week **was** great.*
*The Romans **had** a huge empire.*
*I **believed** in fairies when I was little.*

TIP

Some typical time expressions with the past simple are *yesterday, last week/ year, a week/month ago, the other day/week, at ten o'clock, on Monday, in 2001, once, then, next, after that*.

30 The present perfect

Form

A The present perfect is the present tense of *have* + past participle.

*I've **washed** the dishes.*

*The programme **has finished**.*

For pronunciation and spelling of the ed-form, ➤ 177B, 178B.

Some past participles are irregular.

*We've **seen** this film before.*

*My friends have just **left**.*

For a list of irregular verbs, ➤ page 362.

B In the negative we use *not* or *n't*.

*The dogs **have not eaten** their food.*

*The post **hasn't come** yet.*

In questions we put *have* or *has* before the subject.

*How long **have** you **worked** here?*

***Has** Sarah **passed** her exam?*

Use

C When we use the present perfect, we look back from the present. For example, we can use the present perfect for an action in a period leading up to the present.

*The café **has** just **opened**.*

(It is open **now**.)

*The visitors **have arrived**.*

(They are here **now**.)

The period of time referred to by the present perfect can be very long. It can cover the whole of history or the whole of someone's life up to the present.

> There **have** always **been** wars.
> **Have** you ever **ridden** a horse?

D We can use the present perfect for a series of actions before now.

> I**'ve ridden** horses lots of times.
> We**'ve** often **talked** about moving.

We can also use the present perfect for a state lasting up to the present.

> The film **has been** on for about a week.
> I**'ve had** this computer for three years.

E Some typical time phrases with the present perfect are *just*, *recently*, *lately*, *yet*, *still*, *already*, *before*, *so far*, *ever/never*, *today*, *for weeks/years*, *since 1998*. For *yet*, *still*, and *already*,
> 125B–D.

For more details of time phrases with the present perfect and simple past,
> 32.

TIP

In American English, the past simple is sometimes used when in British English the present perfect would be used, e.g. *I just **saw** something very strange.* **Did** *you ever **meet** anyone famous?*

---

31 Past simple or present perfect?

A Actions

The choice of tense depends on whether the speaker sees something as in the past or linked to the present.

- Past: *The car **broke** down yesterday.*
- Present: *The car **has broken** down.*
  (So it is out of action **now**.)

We use the past simple for a finished time. *The car **broke** down* does not tell us about the present – it may be all right now, or it may be still out of action.

The present perfect makes a link to the present. *The car **has broken** down* tells us that it is out of action now.

When we refer to a specific time in the past (e.g. *yesterday*), we use the past simple rather than the present perfect.

B States

If a state is over, we use the past.
*I **had that** motorbike for years.*
(Then I sold it.)
*I **was there** from three o'clock to five.*
(Then I left.)

If the state still exists now, we use the present perfect.
*I've **had this** motorbike for years.*
*I've **been here** since three o'clock.*

C Repeated actions

When we use the past simple for repeated actions, it means that the series of actions is over.

*Gayle **acted** in more than fifty films.*
(Her career is over.)
*Gayle **has acted** in more than fifty films.*
(Her career has continued up to the present and may or may not be over.)

D Reporting news

We often use the present perfect when we first tell some news, and then we use the past simple for the details such as when and how it happened.

*There **has been** a serious accident on the M6. It **happened** at ten o'clock this morning when a lorry **went** out of control and **collided** with a car.*

The same thing happens in conversation.

*I've just **been** on holiday. ~ Oh, where **did** you go?*
*The new chairs **have arrived**. They **came** yesterday morning.*

TIP

The present perfect is often (but not always) used for recent events. The important thing is that we see the action or state as relevant to the present or in a period that includes the present.

32 Past simple and present perfect: time phrases

A *Just*, *recently*, and *already*

We use *just* and *recently* with either tense with little difference in meaning.

I've just heard the news.

I just heard the news.

There can be a difference with *already*.

I've already heard. (before now)

I already knew yesterday. (before then)

B *Once*, etc and *ever*, *never*

Once, *twice*, etc with the present perfect means the number of times up to now.

We've only been to Scotland once. ~
We've been there at least three times.

With the past simple *once* usually means one occasion in the past.

We went to Scotland once – in 2002.

Ever or *never* with the present perfect means 'in all the time up to now'.

I've never done white water rafting.

Have you ever visited our showroom?

The past simple means a finished period.

Did you ever visit our old showroom?

C *This morning*, *this week*, etc

Look at these examples.

It has been windy this morning.
(The morning is not yet over.)

*It **was** windy **this morning**.*
(It is now afternoon or evening.)

We usually use the present perfect for
a period not yet over.
*I've **watched** a lot of sport **this week**.*
But we use the past simple for one
time during the period.
*I **watched** a great game **this week**.*
(earlier in the same week)

We often use the negative with an
unfinished time.
*It **hasn't been**/It **wasn't** cold **today**.*

D *For* and *since*

We often use *for* and *since* with the
present perfect to express a state.
*He's **been** ill **for** two days / **since** Monday.*

We use *for* with the past simple to say
how long something went on.
*The man **stood** there **for** a moment.*
*We **walked for** hours that day.*

We use *for* and *since* with the negative
present perfect to say when something
last happened.
*I **haven't skied for** years / **since** 2003.*

TIP

To say when something last happened,
we can also use *It's ... since ...* with
either tense, e.g. *It's years since I've
skied* or *It's years since I last **skied**.*

③③The past continuous

A Form

The past continuous is the past of
be + ing-form.

*It **was getting** dark.*
*People **were going** home from work.*
*My mobile **wasn't working**.*
*What **were** you **thinking** about?*

B Basic uses

We use the past continuous to express
the idea that at a time in the past we
were in the middle of something.

*At 3 a.m. I **was lying** there wide awake.*
*The pub was full of people who **were** all
watching football on a big screen.*
*We stood there horrified. Water **was
pouring** through a hole in the ceiling.*

Compare the present continuous and
past continuous.

I'm travelling around the world.
*(I **am** in the middle of my journey.)*
*I **was travelling** around the world.*
*(I **was** in the middle of my journey.)*

We sometimes use the past continuous
for an action going on over a whole
period.

*The builders **were working** all night.*
We could also use the past simple
(*worked*) here.

C Past continuous and simple

An action in the past continuous can happen around a time or around another action.

It **was raining** at ten o'clock.
It **was raining** when I left.

The past continuous is the longer action (the rain falling), and the past simple is the shorter, complete action (my leaving). The shorter action 'interrupts' the longer one.

I **was washing** my hair when you **rang**.
While we **were waiting**, a man **came** in.

But when one complete action followed another, we use the past simple for both.

The bell **rang**, and Tim **went** to the door.

D Past states

For a past state we normally use the simple.

The woman **had** long dark hair.
My grandmother **loved** this house.
(NOT ~~She was loving this house.~~)

Some verbs can be either simple or continuous for a temporary state. ➤ 36B

The men **wore/were wearing** masks.

TIP

Use the past simple for the main action and the continuous for the background, e.g. The sun **was shining**. We **walked** along the beach. People **were lying** in the sun. Children **were playing**.

34 The present perfect continuous

A Form

The present perfect continuous is the present of *have* + *been* + ing-form.

*The game **has been going** on for ages.*
*You **haven't been revising** enough.*
*How long **have** you **been working** here?*

B Use

We use the present perfect continuous for an action over a period of time leading up to the present.

Where have you been? I've been waiting here for half an hour.
*It's wet here. The roof **has been leaking**.*

We do not use the present simple.
NOT *I wait here for half an hour.*

The action can be continuing in the present.

I'm waiting for Tom. I've been waiting ages. (I am still waiting.)

Or the action may have ended recently.

I'm hot because I've been running.
(I stopped running a short time ago.)

We often use *for* and *since*. ➤ 140

We've been living here for six months / since April.

We can also use this tense for a series of repeated actions.

I've been going to evening classes.

C Present perfect or present perfect continuous?

Present perfect	Present perfect continuous
• the result of an action I've **washed** the car, so it's a lot cleaner now.	• an action going on up to the present I've **been washing** the car, so I'm rather wet.
• how much/many Tina **has written** twelve pages of her report.	• how long Tina **has been writing** her report since two o'clock.
• repeated actions I've **been trying** to phone all day.	• how many actions I've **tried** to phone at least twenty times.
• a state up to the present My friend **has been** in hospital for a month.	(We do not use the continuous for a state.)

Note that with *live* and *work*, either form is possible,
e.g. I've **been living** here since May or I've **lived** here since May.
The continuous is more usual.

35 Past perfect tenses

A Past perfect

The past perfect is *had* + past participle.
*Adam was sad that his aunt **had died**.*
*I couldn't go as I **hadn't bought** a ticket.*
*How long **had** the animals **been**
without food and water?*
We use the past perfect for an action
or state before a past time.

Compare the present and past perfect.
*The floor **is** clean. I'**ve washed** it.*
*The floor **was** clean. I'**d washed** it.*

B Past simple and past perfect

We use the past simple for a single
past action or when one action
immediately follows another.
*This bike is new. I **bought** it last week.*
*When the bomb **went** off, the building
collapsed.*

We use *when ... had done* or *after
... did/had done* when one action
followed another.
*When Max **had typed** the message, he
mailed it.* OR *After Max **typed** / Max
had typed the message, he mailed it.*

Compare these examples.
*When I arrived, the meeting **began**.*
(I arrived and then the meeting began.)
*When I arrived, the meeting **had begun**.*
(The meeting began before I arrived.)

C The past perfect continuous

This tense is *had been* + ing-form.
> *Someone **had been using** my computer.*
> *Until then things **hadn't been going** well.*
> ***Had** you already **been practising**?*

We use the past perfect continuous for an action that went on over a period before a past time.
> *When I found the file, **I'd been looking** for it for some time.*

The action of looking went on for some time before the discovery of the file.

D Comparison of tenses

Compare these pairs of sentences.
> *I'm tired. **I've been working**.*
> *I was tired. **I'd been working**.*
> *The volunteers **had collected** hundreds of pounds.* (result of the action)
> *The volunteers **had been collecting** money all morning.* (the action going on)
> *When I saw Alice, she **was playing** golf.* (I saw her in the middle of the game.)
> *When I saw Alice she **'d been playing** golf.* (I saw her after the game.)

TIP

We can use the past perfect after *before* or *until*, e.g. *I felt tired before I **started** / I **had started*** and *We didn't want to stop until we **finished** / we **had finished** the job.*

36 Actions and states

A Action verbs refer to things happening.
  *We **played** football. I'm **buying** a CD.*
Some verbs of reporting and thinking,
e.g. *say, decide,* are also action verbs.
  *I **said** no. You must **decide** soon.*

State verbs express ideas such as being
or knowing, things staying the same.
  *Jane **was** tired. I **know** the answer.*
  *It **belongs** to me. We **need** some help.*

B Action verbs can be continuous; state
verbs cannot usually be continuous.
  *We **are decorating** the flat.*
  NOT ~~We are owning the flat.~~
  *They **were guessing** the answers.*
  NOT ~~They were knowing the answers.~~

Sometimes we can use the continuous
for temporary feelings.
  *I **love** holidays.* (permanent attitude)
  *I'm **loving** this holiday.* (at present)

These verbs can have either form: *feel,
hope, hurt, lie, look* (= appear), *wear.*
  *I **feel** depressed. / I'm **feeling** depressed.*

C For seeing, hearing, etc, we often use *can.*
  *I **can see** a light. We **could hear** music.*
But we use the past simple for a
complete action.
  *We **saw** a show. I **heard** the discussion.*

D Some verbs have more than one meaning. One can be an action and the other a state.

Actions (can be continuous)	States (cannot be continuous)
We're **having** lunch now. ('eating')	We **have** a big kitchen. ('own')
We're **thinking** about it. ('deciding')	I **think** you're right. ('believe')
They're **expecting** some news. ('waiting for it')	I **expect** so. ('believe')
Nurses **care** for the sick. ('look after')	I **don't care** who knows. ('have no feelings')
He was **looking** at Amy. ('directing his eyes at')	This room **looks** lovely. ('has a nice appearance')
Would you like to **taste** the soup? ('eat a little')	It **tasted** like water. ('had a flavour')
Let's **measure** the door. ('find out the size')	It **measured** 2 metres. ('was 2 metres long')
I can **weigh** the luggage. ('find out the weight')	It **weighed** 6 kilos. ('was 6 kilos in weight')
We'll **cost** the project. ('work out the cost')	A ticket **costs** £10. ('has a price of £10')
I was **fitting** a new switch. ('putting in place')	The coat **fits** perfectly. ('is the right size')

Note that *enjoy* is an action verb. Say *I enjoy parties* and
I'm enjoying this party, but not *I enjoy this party*.

73

Overview of verb tenses

Present simple
I **play**

a present state	I **like** old films.
a fact	Cardiff **is** in Wales.
a permanent routine	I **work** late most days.

Present continuous
I **am playing**

| in the middle of an action | I'm **watching** this film. |
| a temporary routine | I'm **working** late this week. |

Present perfect
I **have played**

an action in a period up to now	I've **written** the letter.
a series of actions up to now	I've **played** basketball a few times.
a state in a period up to now	I've **been** here for a week.

Present perfect continuous
I **have been playing**

| an action over a period up to now | It **has been raining** all day. |

Past simple I **played**	an action in the past a past state a series of past actions	I **wrote** the letter yesterday. I **was** there for a week. I **played** basketball regularly at one time.
Past continuous I **was playing**	an action over a period of past time	It **was raining** when I got up.
Past perfect I **had played**	an action before a past time a state before a past time	When we got there, the rain **had stopped**. The weather **had been** awful for days.
Past perfect continuous I **had been playing**	an action over a period up to a past time	When the match started, it **had been raining** for hours.

Each of these verbs forms is either present or past. It can be continuous (*be* + ing-form)
or perfect (*have* + past participle), or it can be both continuous and perfect (*have* + *been*
+ ing-form). But some verbs cannot be used in the continuous. ➤ 36

38 *Will* and *shall*

A Form

After *will* we use an infinitive without to. *Will* and *will not* have short forms '*ll* and *won't*.

*This book **will change** your life.*
*We'**ll know** the results soon.*
*You **won't get** another chance.*
***Will** you **be** in tomorrow?*

After *I* or *we*, either *will* or *shall* can be used. *Shall* is a little formal.

*I **will be** / I **shall be** at home tomorrow.*

B *Will* for the future

Will often refers to things in the future that we can be fairly sure about.

*The South **will stay** dry at the weekend.*
*I'**ll be** 25 next year.*

Will does not express a wish or intention.

We can also use *will* with *have to*, *be allowed to*, and *be able to*.

*We're late. We'**ll have to** hurry.*

C An instant decision

We can sometimes use *I'll / we'll* for an instant decision.

*It's raining. I'**ll take** an umbrella.*

Compare *will* and *be going to*.

*What do I need? Oh, I'**ll buy** a paper.*
(I'm deciding now to buy one.)
*I'**m going to buy** a paper. I won't be long.* (I've already decided to buy one.)

76

D Willingness

Will sometimes expresses willingness.
> *My Polish friend* **will translate** *it for you.*
> *I'll sit / I'm willing to sit on the floor.*

Won't or *will not* can express
unwillingness or an emphatic refusal
to do something.
> *The minister* **will not agree** *to the plan.*
> *I* **won't listen** *to this nonsense.*

E Other uses of *will*

We use *will* for offers and promises.
> *I'll hold the door open for you.*
> *(I promise) I'll do my best to help you.*

F *Shall I/we* or *Will I/we...*?

We use *shall I/we* to offer, or to ask for
advice or suggestions.
> **Shall I carry** *that for you?* ~ *Oh, thanks.*
> *Where* **shall I** *put these flowers?*
> *What* **shall we** *do this weekend?*

But we use *will I/we* for the future.
> **Will I** *need a visa?*
> *When* **will we** *get our results?*

We can use *shall we* for a suggestion.
> **Shall we** *go / Let's go out somewhere?*

TIP

Do not confuse *will* and *want*. Compare
I'll sit down on this seat (a decision) with
*I want to sit down, but there aren't any
seats* (a wish).

39 Be going to

A Form

The form is *be going to* + verb.

I'm going to watch television.
It *isn't going to rain*, is it?
Are you going to buy a ticket?

B *Be going to* for the future

We can use *be going to* for something in the future.

It's going to be fine next week.
I think United *are going to win*.
My father *is* probably *going to be* in hospital for at least two weeks.

Will is also possible in these examples.

Be going to has a sense of something in the present pointing to the future.

It's ten already. We're going to be late.
This wall *is going to fall* down soon.

We can see from the time now that we are going to be late, and we can see from the condition of the wall now that it is going to fall down.

C Intentions

We can use *be going to* for a plan or an intention.

They're going to build a house here.
I'm going to start my own business.

This means that I intend to start / I have decided to start it.

With verbs of movement, especially
go and *come*, we often use the present
continuous rather than *be going to*.
   I'm going out in a minute.
   Of course we're coming to your party.

D *Was going to*

We can use *was/were going to* for a
prediction or an intention in the past.
   I knew there was going to be trouble.
   *I was going to do some shopping, so I
   took my credit card with me.*
This means that I intended to do some
shopping.

Sometimes the intended action does
not actually happen.
   *The bus pulled away just as we **were
   going to get** on it.*
We did not get on the bus because it
pulled away too soon.

Sometimes we can also use *would* for a
past prediction.
   *I knew there **would be** trouble.*
   *I thought that question **would come** up
   in the exam.*

TIP

Was going to is useful when you
are explaining that you meant to do
something but didn't actually do it,
e.g. *I'm sorry. I was going to finish the
report, but I really didn't have time.*

40 Present tenses for the future

A The present continuous

We use the present continuous for
what someone has arranged to do.

I'm meeting Kate at the club tonight.
What are you doing tomorrow?
Julie is going to Florida next month.

This suggests that Julie has made
arrangements such as buying her ticket.

The meaning is similar to *be going
to* for an intention. We can often use
either form.

We're visiting / We're going to visit
friends at the weekend.

B The present simple

We can sometimes use the present
simple for the future when we are
talking about a timetable.

The meeting is on May 13.
The train leaves in five minutes.
What time do you arrive in New York?

We do not use the present simple for
decisions or intentions.

I'll carry that for you.
(NOT *I carry that for you.*)
They're going to build a road through
here soon.
(NOT *They build a road through here*
soon.)

C The present tense in a sub-clause

We often use the present simple for future time in a clause with *if, when, as, while, before, after, until, by the time,* or *as soon as.* This happens when both clauses are about the future.

*If we **meet** at seven, we'll be in time.*
My dad is going to retire when he's sixty.
*Let's wait until the rain **stops**.*
*Call me as soon as you **have** any news.*
(NOT ... ~~as soon as you'll have any news.~~)

The same thing happens in a relative clause or noun clause.

*There will be a prize for the person who **scores** the most points.*
*Make sure everything **is** left tidy, will you?*

We also use the present, and not *will*, with the continuous and the perfect.

*I'll relax when I'm **lying** by the pool.*
(NOT ... ~~when I'll be lying by the pool.~~)
*Let's carry on until we've **finished**.*
(NOT ... ~~until we'll have finished.~~)

TIP

If the main clause has a present-tense verb such as *I expect*, then we do not use another present-tense verb for the future. We say *I expect the rain will stop soon,* not *I expect the rain stops soon.*

41 *Will*, *be going to*, or the present tense?

A There is no single 'future tense' in English. There are a number of different forms we can use for the future, e.g. *will* and *be going to*. There is often more than one possible form in a particular context.

B We use both *will* and *be going to* for the future.

> *It'll* probably **rain** at the weekend.
> Look at those clouds. *It's going to rain*.

The prediction with *be going to* is based on the present situation.

We use *be going to* (not *will*) when the future action seems certain to happen and is very close.

> Help! *I'm going to fall*!
> *I'm going to be* sick!

Sometimes we can use either form.

> *I won't be* / *I'm not going to be* late.
> One day the sun **will cool** down / the sun **is going to cool** down.

C When we talk about intentions, plans, and arrangements, we use *be going to* or the present continuous, but not *will*.

> *We're going to eat* out tonight.
> (We intend to eat out.)

We're eating out tonight.
(We have arranged to eat out.)

Will has a different meaning.
I don't feel like cooking tonight. ~ Well,
we'll eat out then.
Here *will* expresses an instant decision
rather than an existing intention.

We use the present simple for a timetable
but not for an intention or arrangement.
The play starts at seven thirty.
BUT NOT *I act in a play next week.*

D We do not use *will* to first mention a
plan, but we often use it for further
details and comments.
I'm going on holiday on Saturday. I'll
be away for three weeks.
We're going to do some walking. ~ Oh,
that'll be nice.
They're going to lay a new path. The
work will take a couple of days.

Note that we do not use the ordinary
verb *be* in the present continuous.
I'll be away for three weeks.
(NOT *I'm being away for three weeks.*)

TIP

Don't automatically use *will* for the
future. Remember that *be going to*
can be used for both predictions and
intentions, so it is often the safest
choice, especially in conversation.

---

42 Be to, be about to, etc

A Be to for an arrangement

We can use *be* + to-infinitive for an official arrangement.

*The Prime Minister **is to visit** Rome.*
*The two companies **are to merge** shortly.*

Be is often left out in news headlines.

*Prime Minister **to visit** Rome.*

B Be to for an order

Be to can also express a rule or an order by a person in authority.

*The teacher says we **are to wait** here.*
*You**'re not to stay** up late.*
*No one **is to leave** this building.*

C Be about to and be on the point of

We use *be about to* for the near future.

*The performance **is about to start**.*
*Hurry up. The bus **is about to leave**.*

We can use *just* with *be about to* and *be going to* for the very near future.

*The bus **is just about to leave** / **is just going to leave**.*

Be on the point of means the same as *be about to*. It is followed by an ing-form.

*I**'m on the point of quitting** my job.*

There is no time with these phrases.

NOT *We're about to leave in ten minutes.*

D *Be due to*

We can sometimes use *be due* + to-
infinitive to talk about a timetable.
> The meeting **is due to take** place today.
> The train **is due to leave** at 4.20.

E *Be set to*

Be set + to-infinitive is used in news
reports for things expected to happen
soon.
> The player **is set to leave** the club.
> Prices **are set to rise** once more.

F *Be bound/sure/certain to*

We use these forms to say what will
definitely happen in the future.
> There**'s bound to be** trouble.
> The president **is sure/certain to** resign.

G *Was to, was about to, etc*

We can use the forms in the past tense.
> Daniel fell ill on the day he **was to go**
> for a job interview.
> We saw that the bus **was about to leave**.
> We **were on the point of buying** the
> flat when we had second thoughts.

TIP

It is more important to recognize these
forms than to use them. You can express
most of the meanings differently, e.g.
*They have **arranged** to meet. We're going
to leave **in a moment**. There will
definitely be trouble.*

---

43 The future continuous and perfect

A Future continuous

The form is *will be* + ing-form.
I'll be working all day tomorrow.
We won't be doing much on Sunday.
Will you be staying here long?

We use the future continuous for an action that we will be in the middle of.
In a week's time I'll be lying in the sun.
We'll be having tea at seven.
We sometimes use it for an action over a whole future period.
Sarah will be revising all evening.

We also use the future continuous for an action which will result from a routine or arrangement.
I'll be phoning my mother tonight.
(It's part of my regular routine.)
The Queen will be arriving soon.
(It's part of her schedule.)
Other forms are possible in this context.
I'm going to phone / I'm phoning tonight.

B Future perfect

The form is *will have* + past participle.
We'll have done half the job soon.
I won't have got home by six.
How long will the casserole have been in the oven?

We use the future perfect to talk about something being over in the future.

I'll have finished this book soon. I'm nearly at the end.

Gemma won't have completed her studies until she's 25.

C Future perfect continuous

The form is *will have been* + ing-form.

Mike is leaving next month. He'll have been working here ten years.

Our neighbours are moving. They won't have been living here long.

How long will the spaceship have been orbiting the earth?

We use this form when we imagine looking back from the future. In the first example, we look back from next month at Mike's work continuing up to that time.

The future perfect focuses on the result of an action.

I'll have written the report by six.

The future perfect continuous focuses on the action going on.

I'll have been writing it for a week.

TIP

You can use the future continuous to ask about someone's plans and see if they fit in with your wishes, e.g. *How long will you be using the tennis court?*

44 The verb *be*

A We can use *be* as an auxiliary verb.
   I'm surfing the net.
   The information is updated daily.
   Be is used to form the continuous (*am surfing*) and the passive (*is updated*).

B *Be* is more often an ordinary verb.
   The weather is marvellous.
   The talk was quite interesting.
   It can be perfect or continuous.
   The weather has been marvellous.
   You're being very helpful.
   And we can use *be* after a modal verb.
   I might be a bit late tomorrow.

C These are the simple-tense forms.
   Present:
   I am, you/we/they are, he/she/it is
   Past:
   I/he/she/it was, you/we/they were

   We do not use *do* in simple tense negatives and questions.
   It isn't very far now.
   (NOT *It doesn't be very far now.*)
   Were you at the meeting?
   (NOT *Did you be at the meeting?*)

   In other tenses we form negatives and questions in the usual way.
   I haven't been very well.
   How have you been?

D We use the ordinary verb *be* in different ways, for example to talk about someone's identity, nationality, or job, to talk about place and time, and to describe qualities, feelings, and behaviour.

> *Those girls **are** my cousins.*
> *My sister **is** a doctor.*
> *The museum **is** in South Kensington.*
> *The match **was** last Saturday.*
> *That building **is** really ugly.*
> *I**'m** cold and hungry.*
> *Please **be** careful.*

E We can use *be* in the continuous for temporary behaviour.

> *The neighbours **are being** noisy today.*
> *The children **were being** silly.*

Compare these two sentences.

> *You**'re being** stupid.* (behaving stupidly)
> *You**'re** stupid.* (a stupid person)

F *Been* can be a past participle of *go* as well as *be*. Compare these examples.

> *Tom has **been** to town. He got back half an hour ago.*
> *Tom has **gone** to town – he isn't back yet.*

Here *been* means 'gone and come back'. *Gone* means 'gone and still away'.

TIP

In questions about what places people have visited, we use *been*, e.g. *Have you ever been to Africa?*

89

45 The verb *have*

A We can use *have* as an auxiliary verb to form the perfect.
> The computer **has** crashed.
> I **had** already packed a suitcase.

B We use *have* and *have got* to express possession and other related meanings.
> I once **had** a dog.
> Kate **has got** blue eyes.

C In the present we normally use *has got* or *have got*.
> Adam**'s got** the key.
> My neighbours **have got** a balcony.

These sentences are more usual than *Adam has the key* or *They have a balcony*, especially in everyday conversation.

We form negatives and questions in two different ways.
> Adam **hasn't got** the key.
> Adam **doesn't have** the key.
> **Have** you **got** a balcony?
> **Do** you **have** a balcony?

Americans prefer to use the *do* pattern.

D In the past we normally use *had* rather than *had got*.
> I **had** a headache yesterday.
> Our hotel **had** a swimming pool.

Negatives and questions are with *do*.
> *I **didn't have** a headache.*
> ***Did** the hotel **have** a pool?*
> *Had the hotel got a pool?* is less usual.

E We can also use *have* with the perfect and in the to-infinitive or ing-form.
> *I've **had** these shoes for years.*
> *It would be nice **to have** more money.*
> *It's depressing **having** no job.*

We do not use *got* in these patterns.

We do not use the continuous to talk about possession.
> NOT ~~They are having a balcony.~~

F We can use *have* as an action verb with all the tenses, including the continuous.
> *We're **having** fun.* (experiencing)
> *I've **had** lots of presents.* (received)
> *Lucy always **has** toast at breakfast.* (eats)
> *My father **has** a sleep after lunch.* (*has a sleep* = sleeps, ➤ 47)

We use *do* as a simple-tense auxiliary.
> *We **don't have** breakfast on Sundays.*
> ***Did** you **have** a good journey?*

We cannot use *got* with the ordinary verb.
> NOT ~~We've got a great time.~~

TIP

For possession, use *I've got ...* and *Have you got ...?* for the present and *I had ...* and *Did you have ...?* for the past.

46 The verbs *do* and *make*

A We can use *do* as an auxiliary verb in simple tenses.

*I **don't** work on Saturdays.*
*What time **did** you get up?*
*It **does** feel cold.* ➤ 25B

B *Do* can also be an ordinary verb.

*I'm **doing** the crossword.*
*We **did** badly in the quiz.*
*You **haven't done** anything wrong.*
*What on earth **were** you **doing**?*
***Did** everyone **do** it right?*

C We use the ordinary verb *do* when we do not say what the action is.

*What are you **doing**? ~ Writing a poem.*
*Let's **do** something more interesting.*
*Guess what we **did** yesterday.*

We also use *do* to mean 'carry out' or 'complete'.

***Have** you **done** your homework?*
*We **did** the job in less than an hour.*
Do can replace another verb in the context of a task or a service.

*I've **done** the report.* (= written)
*The café **does** Sunday lunches.* (= serves)

We can also use *do* with an ing-form.

*We ought to **do some cleaning** in here.*
*I **did a lot of skiing** last year.* ➤ 78B

D We use the ordinary verb *do* to stand for an action, or when we talk about doing a task.

*I'm afraid I've **done** something silly.*
*We're just **doing** the washing-up.*

The basic meaning of *make* is 'produce' or 'create'.

*I **was** just **making** a cup of tea.*
*The company **makes** a small profit.*

Here are some patterns with *make*.

- *Make* + object
  *Tom **made this table**.*
- *Make* + two objects
  *Tom **made me this table**.*
- *Make* + complement
  *A week in Ireland would **make a nice break**.* (*make* = be)
- *Make* + object + complement
  *The music **made me sad**.*
  (= caused me to become sad)
- *Make* + object + infinitive without *to*
  *The music **made me cry**.*
  (= caused me to cry)

There are many idiomatic uses of *do* and *make*, e.g. you **do** your work, you **do** a course or a subject, you **do** your best, and you **make** sure you don't **make** a mistake.

TIP

A useful idiom is *to do with* meaning 'connected with', e.g. *The boss wants to see you. It's something **to do with** an e-mail.*

---

4 *Have a look*, etc

A Compare these sentences.
> We often **swim** in the pool.
> We often **have a swim** in the pool.

The two sentences have a very similar meaning. We can express some actions as a verb (*swim*) or as an idiom consisting of a verb + object (*have a swim*).

B *Have* is often used in these idioms, but with some we use a different verb such as *make*.
> One of the guests **complained**.
> One of the guests **made a complaint**.

Have, make, etc are ordinary verbs and can be continuous.
> Someone **is having** a swim.

C Here are some idioms of this kind.

Verb	Idiom
act	*take action*
affect	*have an effect on*
argue	*have an argument*
choose	*make a choice*
complain	*make a complaint*
contact	*make contact with*
control	*have/take control of*
decide	*take/make a decision*
describe	*give a description of*
discuss	*have a discussion about*

drink	*have a drink*
	have something to drink
eat	*have a meal*
	have something to eat
guess	*have a guess*
hold	*take/have/keep hold of*
look	*have/take a look*
move	*make a move*
rest	*have a rest*
revise	*do some revision*
sleep	*have a sleep*
start	*make a start*
suggest	*make a suggestion*
swim	*have a swim*
	go for a swim
talk to	*have a talk with*
think	*have a think*
try	*have a try / make an effort*
use	*make use of*
walk	*have/take a walk*
	go for a walk
wash	*have a wash*
work	*do some work*

D Compare the use of the adverb and
adjective in these sentences.
Adverb: *I washed **quickly**.*
Adjective: *I had a **quick** wash.*

TIP

The pattern with the adjective is usually
neater. *She made **good** use of the
computer* sounds much better than *She
used the computer **well**.*

48 Modal verbs

A The modal verbs are *can*, *could*, *must*, *should*, *ought*, *may*, *might*, *will*, *would*, and *shall*. They express ideas such as ability, necessity, and possibility. A modal verb always has the same form and never has an ending such as -*s*, -*ing*, or -*ed*.

B After a modal verb we put an infinitive without *to*.
  We **can park** here. I **must go** now.
The only exception is *ought*.
  I **ought to go** now.

The infinitive can also be perfect, continuous, or passive.
  I **may have shown** you this before.
  They **may be showing** the film soon.
  We **may be shown** the results later.

C To form the negative we use *not* or *n't* with the modal verb.
  It **might not** work. We **shouldn't** laugh.
In questions we put the modal verb before the subject.
  Can we park here?
  (NOT ~~Do we can park here?~~)

D The verbs *need* (➤ 51A–B) and *dare* (➤ 58D) can be used either as modal verbs or as ordinary verbs.
  You **needn't** go. / You **don't need to** go.

96

E Here are some meanings expressed by modal verbs.

Use	Example
Necessity	You **must** be careful. ➤ 50
No necessity	We **needn't** hurry - there's plenty of time. ➤ 51
The right thing to do	You **should** revise / You **ought** to revise before the exam. ➤ 52
Permission	**Can/May** I ask you a personal question?
	We **couldn't** look round without a guide. ➤ 53
Certainty	You **must** be tired after that long walk.
	You **can't** be tired already. ➤ 54
Possibility	I'm not sure, but I **may/might** go out later.
	We **could** go out later if you like. ➤ 55
Ability	Joshua **can** walk on his hands.
	No one **could** hit the target. ➤ 56
Hypothesis	A million pounds **would** be very useful to me now. ➤ 57

49 Modal phrases

A There are some phrases like *have to*, *be allowed to*, and *be able to* which have similar meanings to modal verbs.

I **must** go now. / I **have to** go now.
We **couldn't** touch the exhibits / We **weren't allowed to** touch the exhibits.
I **can** look after myself. / I'**m able to** look after myself.

Modal phrases can be used in many more patterns than modal verbs. For example, we can use modal phrases after *will*, and in certain other forms.

After *will*: We'**ll have to** leave early.
(NOT ~~We'll must leave early.~~)
Perfect: I **haven't been able to** find out.
(NOT ~~I haven't can find out.~~)
Continuous: I'**m having to** do two jobs.
(NOT ~~I'm musting do two jobs.~~)
Infinitive: We hope **to be allowed to** vote.
(NOT ~~We hope to may vote.~~)
Ing-form: I hate not **being able to** sleep.
(NOT ~~I hate not canning sleep.~~)

Where it is not possible to use a modal verb, we can use a modal phrase instead.

TIP

We cannot use two modal verbs together, so not ~~I might can go~~. But we can use a phrase like *be able to* or *have to* after the modal verb: *I might be able to go*.

B Here are some examples of modal phrases.

Modal phrase	Example	Meaning
have to	We **had to** phone for help.	Necessity (*must*) ► 50
had better	**I'd better** do some work.	The best thing to do (*must, should*) ► 52C
be supposed to	You're **supposed to** key the number in.	The rule (*must, should*) ► 52D
be allowed to	We're **allowed to** walk on the grass.	Permission (*can, could, may*) ► 53
be able to	They **were able to** save the man's life.	Ability (*can, could*) ► 56
be unable to	We **are unable to** offer this service.	Ability (*can't, couldn't*) ► 56B
wouldn't mind	I **wouldn't mind** going for a walk.	Willingness ► 57D
would rather	**I'd rather** sit in the shade than in the sun.	Preference ► 57E
used to	There **used to** be a cinema here.	The past ► 58A
be going to	The forecast says it's **going to** rain.	The future (*will*) ► 39
be sure to	The plan **is sure to** go wrong.	Prediction (*will definitely*) ► 42F

For more modal phrases referring to the future, e.g. be to, be about to, ► 42.

50 *Must* and *have to*

A *Must* has just one form and is followed by a to-infinitive.

> You **must wear** something smart.

Have to has both present and past forms.

> We **have to** wear something smart.
> David **has to** work on Sundays.
> I **had to** get up early today.

We form negatives and questions with *do*.

> We **don't have to** wear smart clothes.
> What time **did** you **have to** get up?

Have to can be continuous or perfect and has an infinitive and ing-form.

> I'm **having to** do the work of two people.
> We've **had to** make a few changes.
> I don't like **to have to** wait around.
> It's no fun **having to** stand all the way.

B *Must* and *have to* refer to what is necessary now or in the near future.

> I'm really sweaty. I **must** have a shower.
> We **must** make the arrangements soon.
> We **have to** turn left here. It's one-way.
> Mark **has to** take an exam next week.

For the near future we can also use *will have to*.

> I **have to** go / I'll **have to** go out soon.

We sometimes use *must* to recommend something enjoyable.

> You really **must** watch this programme.

C There is a difference in meaning between *must* and *have to*. We normally use *must* when the speaker/writer decides what is necessary, and we use *have to* when the necessity comes from the situation.

> *You **must** wait in the queue.*
> (I'm telling you.)
> *You **have to** wait in the queue.*
> (That's the rule.)
> *I **must** go on a diet. I want to lose weight.*
> *I **have to** go on a diet. Doctor's orders.*

D Instead of *have to*, we can use *have got to*. The meaning is the same.

> *I **have to** fill this form in.*
> *I**'ve got to** fill this form in.*
> ***Does** everyone **have to** register?*
> ***Has** everyone **got to** register?*

Have got to is informal and used mostly in the present simple. In the past *had to* is more usual than *had got to*.

> *I couldn't go out because I **had to** finish my project.*

We do not use *got* in the perfect or continuous, the infinitive, or the ing-form.

TIP

In general it is safer to use *have to* than to use *must*. *Have to* is much more common in speech. Sometimes *must* can sound strange if you use it in the wrong way.

---

5 Don't have to, needn't, and mustn't

A Don't have to and needn't

We use *don't have to* and *needn't* when we say that something is not necessary.

You **don't have to** apologize. It's not your fault.

You **needn't** apologize. It's not your fault.

Don't have to is more usual than *needn't*.

B Need to

There is an ordinary verb *need*, which we can use in positive and negative sentences and in questions. *Need to* means the same as *have to*. To form negatives and questions we use *do*.

- *have to*

  The colours **have to** match.

  The figure **doesn't have to** be exact.

  Do we **have to** book in advance?

- *need to* (ordinary verb)

  The colours **need to** match.

  The figure **doesn't need to** be exact.

  Do we **need to** book in advance?

- *needn't* (modal verb)

  The figure **needn't** be exact.

  BUT NOT ~~The colours need match.~~

  The modal verb *needn't* is normally used only in the negative.

C *Didn't need to do* and *needn't have done*

We use *didn't need to* for an action that didn't happen because it wasn't necessary.

*It was a lovely day. I **didn't need to take** my umbrella, so I left it at home.*

If something happened which we now see was unnecessary, we can use either form.

*I **needn't have brought** / **didn't need to bring** this umbrella with me, but I didn't realize it would be such a lovely day.*

D *Mustn't*

We use *mustn't* to tell someone not to do something or to avoid something.

*You **mustn't** forget your keys,*
*We **mustn't** lose this game.*

Mustn't or *may not* can be used to forbid something.

*Students **must not** / **may not** use dictionaries in the exam.*

TIP

Mustn't has a different meaning from *don't have to* / *needn't*. Use *mustn't* for a necessity not to do something. Use *don't have to* or *needn't* when there is no necessity.
*I **mustn't** run. I've got a weak heart.*
*I **don't have to** / **needn't** run. I've got plenty of time.*

52 *Should, ought to, had better, and be supposed to*

A We use *should* and *ought to* when we say what is the right thing or the best thing to do.

> We **should** recycle / We **ought to** recycle as much as possible.
> You **should** see / You **ought to** see the film. You'll love it.

In negatives and questions we normally use *should*.

> People **shouldn't** leave litter everywhere.
> Who **should** we invite to the wedding?

We can use the continuous or perfect after *should* and *ought to*.

> I **should be doing** some work now.
> You **ought to have said** thank you.

B We can also use *should* to say that something is probable.

> They **should** have my letter by now.
> There's only a short queue, so we **shouldn't** have to wait long.

Should implies 'if all goes well'.

> There are no reports of delays, so the train **should** be on time.

We do not use it for things going wrong.

> The train **will probably** be late.
> (NOT *The train should be late.*)

C *Had better* says what is the best thing
to do in a particular situation.
  *I think James **had better** see a doctor.*
  *I'**d better** tidy up this mess, hadn't I?*
  Had better is stronger than *should* or
  ought to. *I'd better tidy up* means that
  I am going to tidy up because it is the
  best way to deal with the problem.

  The negative is *had better not*.
  *Come on. We'**d better not** be late.*
  *The lorry **had better not** park across
  the entrance.*

D We use *be supposed to* for what
should happen because it is the rule
or the normal way of doing things.
  *You'**re supposed to** wait in the queue.*
  In the negative it means something
  isn't allowed.
  *We'**re not supposed to** keep pets here.*

  Be supposed to can mean that
  something is arranged or intended.
  *I'**m supposed to** be on holiday, but I
  keep getting calls from the office.*
  *How **is** this device **supposed to** work?*

TIP

To talk about what people in general say
or believe, we can use *be supposed to*.
*Too much sugar is supposed to be bad
for you* means that people say too much
sugar is bad for you.

53 Can, could, may, and be allowed to

A Asking permission

We use *can*, *could*, or *may* to ask permission.

> ***Can** I take your umbrella?*
> ***Could** I use this calculator, please?*
> ***May** we come in? ~ Yes, of course.*

Could is less direct than *can* and often more polite. *May* is rather formal.

B Giving/refusing permission

We use *can* or *may* to give permission.

> *You **can** use my mobile if you like.*
> *May I see the letter? ~ Of course you **may**.*

May is more formal.

We use *cannot/can't* to refuse permission.

> *You **can't** have Saturday off. I'm sorry.*

C Talking about permission

To talk about permission when we are not giving it or asking for it, we can use *can* referring to the present or future and *could* referring to the past.

> *I **can** stay up as late as I like.*
> *At one time you **could** park here.*

We do not usually use *may* here.
We can also use *be allowed to*.

> *I'm **allowed to** stay up as late as I like.*
> *Was Tina **allowed to** leave work early?*

Compare these two sentences.

May we leave early please?
(Will you allow it?)
Are we *allowed* to leave early?
(What is the rule?)

We also use *be allowed to* where *can* and *may* are not possible: with *will*, in the perfect or continuous, and in the to-infinitive and ing-form.

You *won't be allowed to* take photos in the museum.
The media *have not been allowed to* report what's been going on.
No one *is being allowed to* occupy any of the buildings.
I expected *to be allowed to* sit down.
It's great *being allowed to* miss lessons.

For general permission in the past, we use *could* or *was/were allowed to*.

Years ago you *could* feed / you *were allowed to* feed the animals.

But for a specific action with permission, we use *was/were allowed to*.

The four children *were allowed to* feed the animals.

TIP

You can answer a request for permission with *(Yes,) of course*. To refuse, you should give a reason, e.g. *Sorry, I'm using it.*

54 *Will*, *must*, and *can't* expressing certainty

A We can use *will* for an assumption.

> *Don't ring Luke now. He'll be at work.*
> *There's someone at the door. ~ It'll be the postman.*

The speaker assumes that the postman is at the door because this is his normal time. *It'll be the postman* is a kind of prediction about the present.

B *Must* can express certainty.

> *You saw the film last week, so you must know what it's about.*
> *Jane got up at four, so she must be tired.*

The speaker sees it as necessarily and logically true that Jane is tired.

We use *can't* for something impossible.

> *This can't be Christopher's textbook. He doesn't do physics.*

Americans use *must not*.

> *This must not be Christopher's textbook.*

We use *can* in questions about what is possible.

> *Who can that be at the door?*
> *Can it really be true?*

Must and *can't* are opposites.

> *The bill can't be so much. There must be a mistake.* (There is certainly a mistake.)

C After *will*, *must*, and *can't* expressing certainty, we can use the continuous.

Where's Carl? ~ He'll be sitting in a café somewhere, I expect.
The bus is late. It must be coming soon.

Compare *must do* and *must be doing*.
You've got exams soon. You must work. (I'm telling you to work.)
Sam isn't at home. He must be working. (So I'm sure he's working.)

We can also use the perfect with *will*, *must*, and *can't*.
Someone must have set off the alarm.
I can't have made a mistake.

We can use the passive with the perfect.
The best seats will have been sold now.
The bike must have been stolen while we were having our lunch.

D We can use *had to* and *couldn't* when something was certain in the past.
The fingerprints were his, so he had to be the murderer. It couldn't be anyone else.

TIP

As well as *must*, we can sometimes use *have (got) to* for logical certainty, e.g. *You've got to be joking!* to convey disbelief. But in general it is safer to use *must* for certainty.

55 *May*, *might*, *can*, and *could*

A We use *may* and *might* for possibility.
   *This old picture **may/might** be valuable.*
   *The shop **may not/might not** be open.*
   This includes their use for an
   uncertain prediction or intention.
   *It **may/might** rain tomorrow.*
   *I **may/might** go away next weekend.*

   We often avoid *may/might* in questions.
   ***Do you think** it'll rain tomorrow?*

B We can use a statement with *could* or
   might to make a suggestion or to express
   criticism that something is not done.
   *You **could/might** listen when I'm
   talking.*
   *You **could/might** have helped us.*

C We use *could* for possibility or for an
   uncertain prediction.
   *This old picture **could** be valuable.*
   *The asteroid **could** hit the earth.*
   We can also use *may* or *might* here but
   not *can*.

   We also use *could* to suggest possible
   future actions.
   *We **could** go for a walk this afternoon.*
   Compare this use of *could* with *may/
   might* for an uncertain intention.
   *We **could** have a party. ~ Yes, why not?*
   *We **may** have a party. ~ Oh, when?*

D We use *can* and *could* in requests.
> ***Can/Could*** *you wait a moment, please?*

We also use *can* to offer help.
> ***Can*** *I give you a lift? ~ Yes, please.*

E We sometimes use *can* for what is
generally possible.
> *You* ***can*** *make wine from bananas.*

We also use *can* for things that
sometimes happen.
> *The motorway* ***can*** *get busy.*
> (It sometimes gets busy.)

Compare *may/might not* with *can't.* ➤ 54B
> *The story* ***can't*** *be true. It must be a lie.*
> (It is impossible that it is true.)
> *The story* ***may not*** *be true. I'm not sure.*
> (It is possible that it is not true.)

F We can use *may*, *might*, and *could*
with the continuous, the perfect, and
the passive.
> *I* ***might be playing*** *badminton tomorrow.*
> *Tina* ***could be working*** *late today.*
> *I* ***may have thrown*** *the leaflet away.*
> *The flight* ***could have been delayed***.
> *He* ***might have been having*** *a shower.*

TIP

Might as well is a useful phrase to say
that there is no better alternative, e.g.
This lamp is useless. I ***might as well***
throw it away.

---

56 Can, could, and be able to

A Can and could

We use *can* to express ability.
> Nicola **can** play chess.
> **Can** you draw a perfect circle?
> We **can't** lift this piano.

The negative of *can* is *cannot*, written as one word. It has a short form *can't*.

We use *could* for ability in the past.
> My grandfather **could** walk on his hands.

As well as physical or mental ability, we also use *can* and *could* for an opportunity to do something.
> We **can** sit in the garden when it's sunny.
> We **couldn't** keep a dog in our old flat.

B Be able to

Am/is/are able to means the same as *can*.
> The pupils **can** read / **are able to** read.

The negative is *not able to* or *unable to*.
> The office **cannot** supply / **is not able to** supply / **is unable to** supply the figures.

We can use *be able to* (but not *can*) in other tenses and forms.
> You **will be able to** check your progress.
> He **hasn't been able to** play for ages.
> It's nice **to be able to** relax.
> **Being able to** speak the language is a great advantage.

C *Could* and *was/were able to*

Both these forms are possible when we talk about a general ability in the past.

*Tracy **could** swim / **was able to** swim when she was a baby.*

But we use *was/were able to* (and not *could*) for a particular situation.

*Firemen **were able to** put out the fire.*
*The man **was able to** call for help.*
(NOT *The man could call for help.*)

He had the ability to call for help (and he did actually call for help).

In negatives and questions either form is possible.

*We **couldn't** get / **weren't able to** get tickets for the show.*
***Could** you find / **Were** you **able** to find it?*

We normally use *could* (not *was/were able to*) with verbs of perception and verbs of thinking.

*We **could see** smoke on the horizon.*
*I **could understand** that you felt upset.*

For a chance not taken, we use *could have*.

*He **could have** run, but he was too lazy.*

TIP

Succeeded in doing and *managed to do* mean the same as *was able to do*, e.g. *Detectives **were able to solve** / **succeeded in solving** / **managed to solve** the mystery.*

113

57 *Would*

A Form

Would has a short form *'d*.
> *Anyone **would** look silly in that hat.*
> *I**'d** look ridiculous wearing that.*

We form negatives and questions in the
same way as other modal verbs. ➤ 48C
> *This colour **wouldn't** suit me, would it?*
> *When **would** I wear it?*

B Use

We use *would* for a possible,
hypothetical situation. Compare:
> *We're going to have a barbecue. ~ Oh,*
> *that**'ll** be nice.* (a future situation)
> *We're thinking of having a barbecue. ~*
> *Oh, that**'d** be nice.* (a possible situation)

With *would* there is often a phrase
or clause explaining the possible
situation.
> *You **wouldn't** be much use **in a crisis**.*
> *No one **would** pay taxes **if they didn't***
> ***have to**.* ➤ 158

C *Would like*

Would like means the same as *want*.
> *Fiona **would like** to work in television.*
> *We**'d like** a place of our own to live.*
We use it in offers and invitations.
> ***Would anyone like** a drink?*
> ***Would you like** to join us for lunch?*

Compare *like* and *would like*.
> *I'm a great dancer. I **like** going / I **like** to go to clubs.* (I always enjoy going.)
> *Let's go out somewhere. I'**d like** to go to a club.* (I want to go.)

We can also use *would* with verbs such as *love*, *hate*, and *enjoy*.
> *Emily **would love** to do deep-sea diving.*
> *I'**d hate** to live in a big city.*

D *Would mind*

We use this in negatives and questions.
> *I **wouldn't mind** watching this film.*
> (I want to watch it.)
> ***Would** you **mind** changing places?*
> (a polite request)

E *Would rather*

Would rather means 'prefer' or 'would prefer'.
> *I'**d rather** walk than wait for a bus.*
> *Karen **would rather** we kept together.*
> ***Would** you **rather** eat now or later?*

It is followed by an infinitive without *to* (*walk*) or by a clause (*we kept together*).

The negative is *would rather not*.
> *I'**d rather not** take any risks.*

TIP

To ask for something, use *would like*, not *want*. *I'd like a drink, please* is more polite than *I want a drink*.

---

58 *Used to* and *dare*

A *Used to*

Used to means that something happened regularly or continued for a time in the past but no longer does so.

> I **used to** come here when I was a child.
> Emma **used to** have a bicycle, but then she sold it.

There is no present-tense form.

NOT ~~I use to come here now.~~

We use *did* in negatives and questions.

> There **didn't use to** be so much crime.
> What **did** people **use to** do before they had television?

We can also use *never* for the negative.

> There **never used to** be so much crime.

B *Used to* and *be/get used to*

Compare these patterns.

> We **used to live** in the country before we moved to London.
> It was strange at first, but we**'re used to living** here now.

Used to do refers to the past, and *be used to doing* means that something no longer feels strange.

Get used to refers to something becoming more familiar.

> If you go to live in France, you'll have to **get used to driving** on the right.

C *Would* for past habits

In literary English, *would* can be used
to talk about past habits.

> *Every day my father **would** leave / used
> to leave the house before I was awake.*

With states only *used to* is possible.

> *We **used to own** a motorboat.*

D *Dare*

Dare can be a modal verb or an
ordinary verb, and it takes an
infinitive with or without *to*.

> *Few people **dare (to)** go out at night.*
> *No one **dares (to)** protest / **dare** protest.*
> *Who **would dare (to)** resist?*
> *One man **had dared (to)** take the risk.*

If you *dare*, you are brave enough, and
if you *daren't*, then you are afraid.

Dare is more common in negatives
and questions. The negative forms are
don't/doesn't/didn't dare or *daren't/dare
not* (present) and *dared not* (past).

> *I **don't dare** look/**daren't** look at the bill.*
> *The police **didn't dare to** approach /
> **dared not** approach the building.*

Questions also have different forms.

> ***Do** you **dare** to try? / **Dare** you try?*

TIP

The *s* in *used* is pronounced /z/ in e.g.
I used my key and /s/ in e.g. *I used to
go fishing* or *I'm used to the noise.*

117

Passive verb forms

A A passive verb has a form of *be* and a passive participle.

	Active	Passive
Present simple	They **play** the game.	The game **is played**.
Present continuous	They **are playing** the game.	The game **is being played**.
Present perfect	They **have played** the game.	The game **has been played**.
Past simple	They **played** the game.	The game **was played**.
Past continuous	They **were playing** the game.	The game **was being played**.
Past perfect	They **had played** the game.	The game **had been played**.
Future	They **will play** the game.	The game **will be played**.
	They **are going to play** the game.	The game **is going to be played**.

We can use short forms, e.g. *It's played every year.*

B Negatives and questions

In the negative *not* comes after the first auxiliary.

*Motorists **are not killed** by cyclists.*

*The money still **hasn't been found**.*

In a question there is inversion of the subject and (first) auxiliary.

***Has** the money **been found**?*

*When **was** the fax **sent**?*

C Modal verbs in the passive

We can use the passive with a modal verb, or with a phrase like *have to*.

*Stamps **can be bought** at any post office.*

*The work once **had to be done** by hand.*

*The note **might have been thrown** out.*

*Animals **shouldn't be kept** in cages.*

***Could** the process **be speeded** up?*

D Phrasal verbs in the passive

Some phrasal and prepositional verbs and verbal idioms can be passive.

*The flats **were knocked down** last year.*

*Has the doctor been **sent for**?*

*Slavery should be **done away with**.*

*The child is always being **made fun of**.*

The adverb or preposition (*down, for,* etc) comes after the participle.

TIP

Be + passive participle can express an action or a state. Compare *The vase was broken by a guest* (action) and *The vase was broken. It lay in pieces.* (state)

60 The use of the passive

A Introduction

Compare the active and passive sentences

Active: Amy **faxed** the report.

Passive: The report **was faxed** by Amy.

We can choose to talk about Amy and what she did, or about the report and what happened to it. This often depends on what is old or new information. ➤ 21

B The agent

When we need to mention the agent in a passive sentence, we use *by*.

*The story was written **by Dickens**.*

But often we mention other information rather than the agent.

*The concert is being held **in the park**.*

*Plugs should be wired **correctly**.*

Often the agent is irrelevant or too obvious to mention.

A new government has been elected.

C Typical contexts

We sometimes use the passive in speech, but it is more common in writing, especially in the impersonal style of textbooks and factual information.

The paint is pumped into a large tank.

The slaves were sold to traders.

Many new jobs have been created.

The focus is on the processes rather than on the people carrying them out.

The passive is also sometimes used for rules and procedures.

The service is provided under a contract.
Application should be made in writing.
The active *You should apply ...* is more friendly and less impersonal.

D *You, we,* etc

In informal English we often avoid the passive (P) by using the active (A) with e.g. *you, we, they, people,* or *someone.*

P: *Nothing can be done about it.*
A: ***You** can't do anything about it.*
P: *Education is valued.*
A: ***We/People** value education.*
P: *The gates have been opened.*
A: ***Someone** has opened the gates.*

E Verbs without passive forms

An intransitive verb (e.g. *happen*) has no object and so cannot be passive. Some state verbs with an object cannot be passive, e.g. *have* (= own), *lack, suit.*

*My friend **has** a sports car.*
(NOT ~~A sports car is had by my friend.~~)
But other state verbs can be passive, e.g. *know, love, need, own, want.*

*Old toys **are wanted** by collectors.*

> **TIP**
> Do not overuse the passive. Use it only when it fits the context and the style. Even in formal writing most clauses are active.

61 Some passive patterns

A *Give, send,* etc

In the active, *give* can have two objects.

*The nurse gives **the patient a pill**.*

Either of these objects can be the subject of a passive sentence.

***A pill** is given to the patient.*

***The patient** is given a pill.*

It is quite usual in English to begin with the person receiving something.

***The speaker** was handed a note.*

I've been offered a job.

***The residents** will be found new homes.*

Some verbs in this pattern are *ask, feed, find, give, hand, lend, offer, pay, promise, sell, send, show, teach, tell.*

B *It is said ...*

We use this pattern with verbs of reporting.

***It is said** that the number 13 is unlucky.*

(People say that 13 is unlucky.)

Here are some more examples.

***It is thought** that the painting is genuine.*

***It was reported** that people were dying.*

Some verbs in this pattern are *accept, agree, announce, argue, assume, believe, claim, decide, expect, feel, find, hope, know, notice, predict, realize, report, say, see, show, state, suggest, think, understand.*

C ... *said to be* ...

This pattern involves a passive verb of reporting and a to-infinitive.

*The number 13 **is said to be** unlucky.*
*We **were expected to win**, but we lost.*

Note these forms of the to-infinitive.

*A crowd was reported **to be gathering**.*
*He is known **to have committed** crimes.*
*A man is believed **to have been killed**.*

Some verbs in this pattern are *assume, believe, claim, expect, feel, find, know, mean, prove, report, say, see, show, state, suppose, think, understand.*

D Passive verb + to-infinitive

We use this pattern with verbs like *tell, persuade, advise, force,* and *allow.* ➤ 68B-C

*Drivers **are advised to avoid** the area.*

Note also *make* (➤ 72D) and *see, hear,* etc (➤ 72E).

*The hostages **were made to lie** down.*
*The man **was seen to run** away.*

E Passive verb + participle

This pattern involves an active participle.

*The man **was seen running** away.*
*We **were kept waiting** half an hour.*

We use *see, hear,* etc (➤ 81A) and *catch, find, keep, leave, lose, spend, waste.*

TIP

Use *allow* in the passive but not *let*, e.g.
*The hostages **were allowed to** go free.*

62 Patterns with *have* and *get*

A The passive with *get*

We sometimes form the passive with *get* rather than with *be*.

*Luckily I **got accepted** at art school.*
*Lots of people **get killed** on the roads.*

The pattern is used mainly in informal English, and it has a more limited use than *be*. We can use *get* to talk about good or bad things happening.

We can also use *get* for something happening incidentally, as part of a larger operation.

*The dustbin **gets emptied** once a week.*

But it is not used for a planned action.

*The railway **was privatized** in the 1990s.*
(NOT *The railway got privatized.*)

We use *do* in simple-tense negatives and questions.

*The bins **didn't get emptied** yesterday.*
*How often **do** rugby players **get injured**?*

B Idioms with *get*

We use *get* + passive participle in some idiomatic expressions.

*I'll have to **get washed**.* (wash myself)
*Ed has **got married**.* (married someone)

These include *get washed, get shaved, get (un)dressed; get engaged, get married, get divorced.*

C *Have/get something done*

This pattern means 'cause something to be done'. We use it mainly to talk about professional services to a customer.

> I **had** my car **serviced**.
> I **got** my car **serviced**.

This means that I arranged for a garage to service my car. *Get* is a little informal.

Here are some more examples.

> We must **have/get** the machine **repaired**.
> Lucy **has had** her kitchen **extended**.
> We're **having/getting** a new tap **fitted**.
> Where **did** you **have/get** your hair **cut**?

We can also use *get* informally for a job we do ourselves.

> I must **get** my homework **done**.
> We **got** everything **packed** and ready.

D *Have something happen*

This pattern has the same form as *have something done* in C. It often refers to an unpleasant experience.

> We **had** a window **broken** in the storm.
> My sister **has had** some money **stolen**.

TIP

Do not confuse *had something done* and *had done something*. If *we had the grass cut*, then someone did it for us. If *we had cut the grass*, then we did it before a time in the past (past perfect ➤ 35A).

The passive to-infinitive and gerund

A Look at these forms of the verb *play.*

	Active	Passive
To-infinitive	to play	to be played
Perfect to-infinitive	to have played	to have been played
Gerund	playing	being played
Perfect gerund	having played	having been played

Here are some examples of the passive forms.

To-infinitive: It's embarrassing **to be criticized** in public.
Perfect to-infinitive: The fire seems **to have been caused** by an electrical fault.
Gerund: **Being searched** by customs officers is not a pleasant experience.
Perfect gerund: There is no record of any message **having been sent.**

B The active gerund has a passive
meaning after *need* or *want* (= need).
*The room needed **decorating**.*
(= The room needed to be decorated.)
We cannot use the passive gerund here.
(NOT *It needed being decorated.*)

C We sometimes use an active to-
infinitive for jobs we have to do.
*We had the living-room **to decorate**.*
*I've got some homework **to do**.*
When the subject (*we, I*) is the person
doing the job, we use the active. But in
other cases, we use the passive.
*The living-room had **to be decorated**.*
*The work is **to be done** by tomorrow.*

After the subject *there*, the infinitive is
either active or passive.
*There's a wall **to paint** / **to be painted**.*
*There's work **to do** / **to be done**.*

After an adjective, we usually use the
active.
*The piano is too **heavy to move**.*
But if we use a phrase with *by*, then the
infinitive is passive.
*The piano is too heavy **to be moved by
one person**.*

TIP

When we talk about leisure activities,
we normally use the active, e.g. *There
are lots of exciting things **to do***.

64 The infinitive

A An infinitive can be with *to* or without *to*.
> I'd prefer **to sit** at the back.
> I'd rather **sit** at the back.

Whether we use *to* depends on the grammatical pattern. For example, we use it after *prefer* but not after *would rather*.

The most common use of an infinitive without *to* is after a modal verb.
> I **can sit** at the back.

For the infinitive without *to*, ➤ 72.

B A to-infinitive can have these forms.
- Simple: *to do*
  > It's great **to see** you.
- Perfect: *to have done*
  > I seem **to have left** my umbrella behind.
- Continuous: *to be doing*
  > You're lucky **to be living** here.
- Perfect + continuous: *to have been doing*
  > A man at the bus stop appeared **to have been drinking**.

For passive forms, ➤ 63A.

In the negative, *not* comes before the infinitive.
> I'd prefer **not to sit** at the front.
> It would have been too risky **not to have had** medical insurance.

C An infinitive can be followed by an object or complement and/or by one or more adverbials. The infinitive together with such phrases is an infinitive clause.

> *A sightseeing tour is the best way **to see the city**.* (infinitive + object)
> *I'm doing my best **to keep fit**.*
> (infinitive + complement)
> *I'd be quite happy **to sit at the back**.*
> (infinitive + adverbial)

Or an infinitive clause can be just an infinitive on its own.

> *We decided **to leave**.*

D In an infinitive clause, a preposition comes in its normal place, often after a verb or adjective.

> *It isn't enough money to live **on**.*
> *There's nothing to get excited **about**.*
> *I need a vase to put these flowers **in**.*

In more formal English the clause can begin with a preposition and relative pronoun.

> *It is not enough money **on which** to live.*

TIP

A one-word adverbial can often go after *to* and before the verb, e.g. *Now we've got a chance to **really** relax.* This is called a 'split infinitive'. A few people think it is incorrect, but in fact it is common usage.

---

65 Some patterns with the to-infinitive

A The to-infinitive with *it*

We often use a pattern with *it* as the subject and an infinitive clause at or near the end of the sentence.

*It seems rude **to refuse the invitation**.*
*It's a mistake **not to take any exercise**.*
*It takes ages **to defrost this fridge**.*

An infinitive clause can sometimes be the subject, but this is less common.

***To refuse the invitation** seems rude.*

B To-infinitive clause as complement

The clause can be a complement after *be*.

*My intention is **to emigrate to Australia**.*
*The important thing is **not to panic**.*

C Purpose

A to-infinitive clause can express purpose.

*Jack went out **to do some shopping**.*
*I am writing **to enquire about courses**.*
***To get a seat**, you need to arrive early.*

In the negative we cannot use a simple to-infinitive.

NOT ~~We were quiet not to disturb you.~~

Instead we use *so as* or *so that*.

*We were quiet **so as not to** disturb you.*
*We were quiet **so that** we **wouldn't** disturb you.*

D Outcome

A to-infinitive clause sometimes
expresses an outcome.

*Laura arrived home from work **to find
her house on fire**.*

*The prince grew **up to be a handsome
young man**.*

We can use *only* to express the idea
that effort has been wasted.

*We all arrived for the concert **only to
find** it had been cancelled.*

E Comment

A to-infinitive clause can express a
comment on the speaker's honesty.

***To tell you the truth**, I've had enough
sightseeing for today.*

Note also *to be (perfectly) frank/honest.*

F *To hear ... / To see ...*

We can use a clause with *to hear* or *to
see* to explain why you could get the
wrong idea.

***To hear him talk**, you'd think he was
God's gift to women.*

***To see her in those old clothes**, you'd
never guess she was fabulously rich.*

TIP

A gerund as subject is more usual than
an infinitive. ***Defrosting** this fridge takes
ages* sounds better than *To defrost this
fridge takes ages.*

---

66 Verb + to-infinitive or gerund?

A We use a to-infinitive after certain verbs.
*I **decided to walk** to the hotel.*
Other verbs take a gerund.
*I **suggested walking** to the hotel.*
Some verbs take either form. ➤ 67

B These verbs take a to-infinitive:
*afford, agree, aim, appear, arrange,
ask, attempt, beg, care, choose, claim,
consent, decide, demand, desire,
be dying, expect, fail, happen, help,
hesitate, hope, learn, long, manage,
offer, plan, prepare, pretend, promise,
prove, refuse, seek, seem, tend,
threaten, turn out, volunteer, vote,
can't wait, want, wish.*

C These verbs take a gerund: *admit,
allow, avoid, consider, delay, deny,
detest, dislike, enjoy, can't face, fancy,
finish, give up, can't help, imagine,
involve, justify, keep, keep on, mind,
miss, postpone, practise, quit, resist,
report, resent, resume, risk, suggest.*

D *Want* + to-infinitive is a common
pattern. *Wish* and *desire* are more formal.
*Do you **want to say** anything?*
*Do you **wish to make** a comment?*
Fancy + gerund is informal.
*Do you **fancy going** out somewhere?*

VERB + TO-INFINITIVE OR GERUND?

E *Look* + to-infinitive can mean 'seem'.
  *The company **looks to be** in difficulties.*
  In the continuous it can mean 'aim to'.
  *United are **looking to win** today.*

F We can use a to-infinitive after *ask*.
  *The customer **asked to see** the manager.*
  Usually there is an object after *ask*.
  *He **asked the manager to sort** the
  problem out.*

G We use *mind* and *care* mainly in
  negatives and questions.
  *I **don't mind walking** if it's fine.*
  ***Would** you **care to come** with us?*

H *Allow* takes a gerund.
  *They don't **allow sunbathing** here.*
  But when it has an object, *allow* takes a
  to-infinitive.
  *They don't **allow you to sunbathe** here.*

I We can use a combination of forms.
  *I'm afraid I **failed to learn to ski**.*
  *I **refuse to risk losing** so much money.*
  *We were **considering offering to help**.*

TIP

We can use *agree* with a to-infinitive,
e.g. *We **agreed to pay** the cost.* But we
cannot do the same with *accept*. We say
*We **accepted that we should pay** the
cost*, not *We accepted to pay the cost*.

133

67 Verbs taking either form

A Some verbs can take either a
to-infinitive or a gerund with no
difference in meaning.

> I **hate to arrive / hate arriving** late.
> We **intend to take / intend taking** action.
> It soon **started to rain / started raining**.

These verbs are: *begin, bother, can't
bear, can't stand, cease, commence,
continue, hate, intend, like, love, prefer,
propose, start.*

B We usually avoid two ing-forms together.

> I was **intending to study** law.
> (NOT ~~I was intending studying law.~~)

After *begin, continue,* and *start,* a state
verb usually has the to-infinitive form.

> I **began to understand** the problems.

C *Like, love,* and *hate* take either form.

> Kate **likes to cook / likes cooking**.
> I **hate to travel / hate travelling** by
> bus.

Like takes a to-infinitive when
something is a good idea rather than a
pleasure.

> I **like to keep** the place tidy.

Would like, would love, and *would hate*
normally take a to-infinitive.

> Our guest **would like to say** something.
> We**'d love to go** on a cruise.

D The to-infinitive and gerund have different meanings after the verbs on this page.

Remember/forget + to-infinitive is about whether we do necessary actions.
> Did you **remember to turn** off the gas?
> You **forgot to sign** the form.

But we use a gerund for memories.
> I can **remember waking** up in the night.
> I'll never **forget running** that marathon.

Regret + to-infinitive is for bad news.
> We **regret to inform** you that your application has been unsuccessful.

Regret + gerund is about the past.
> I **regret wasting** so much time.

Try + to-infinitive means to do your best.
> I'm **trying to light** a fire.

Try + gerund means to see if the action will solve the problem.
> **Try pouring** some petrol on it.

Mean + to-infinitive has the sense of 'intend'.
> Sorry. I didn't **mean to step** on your foot.

Mean + gerund is about a situation making an action necessary.
> An early flight **means getting** up at six.

TIP

Stop takes a gerund, e.g. **Stop dreaming** and do some work. But we can also use a to-infinitive of purpose after *stop*, e.g. I **stopped to buy** a newspaper. ➤ 65C

68 Verb + object + to-infinitive

A Introduction

Some verbs can take an object and a to-infinitive.

*Simon **wants you to ring** him.*
*The host **asked us not to smoke**.*
*I **expected Amy to meet** me.*

The object of the verb (*you, us, Amy*) is also the subject of the to-infinitive, e.g. *Amy* is the subject of *to meet*.

Most of the verbs can be passive.
*We **were asked** not to smoke.*

B *Tell, persuade,* etc

*The doctor **told Julie to stay** in bed.*
*I **persuaded Vicky to come** with me.*

These verbs of ordering and requesting include: *advise, ask, beg, challenge, command, encourage, instruct, invite, order, persuade, remind, request, tell, urge, warn.*

C *Force, allow,* etc

*The humps **force drivers to slow** down.*
*The firm **allows me to work** at home.*

These verbs of causing and permitting include: *allow, assist, authorize, cause, compel, drive, enable, entitle, forbid, force, get, help, inspire, intend, lead, mean, oblige, pay, permit, provoke, require, teach, tempt, train.*

D *Believe, show, etc*

> *We **believe the picture to be** genuine.*
> *The photo **showed the contestant to have broken** the rules.*

These are mainly verbs of thinking.
They include: *assume, believe, consider, declare, discover, expect, feel, find, imagine, know, prove, reveal, show, suppose, suspect, understand.*

This pattern is rather formal. We can often use a that-clause.

> *We **believe** (that) the picture **is** genuine.*

The passive pattern is more common.

> *The picture **is believed to be** genuine.*

Say is used only in the passive. ➤ 61C

> *The project **is said to be** on schedule.*

E *Want, like, etc*

> *We **want people to have** fun.*
> *I'd **like you to be** honest with me.*

This group includes *can't bear, hate, like, love, need, prefer, want, wish.*

We cannot use a that-clause.

> NOT *We want that people have fun.*

And we cannot use the passive.

> NOT *People are wanted to have fun.*

TIP

Do not say *I suggested her to take part.*
Say *I suggested that she should take part.*

69 Adjective + to-infinitive

A A common pattern is *it* + linking verb
+ adjective + to-infinitive clause.
  *It is **easy to answer** the question.*
  *It was **good to see** you again.*
  *It felt **strange to be working** at night.*
Many adjectives can be used, e.g.
*correct, dangerous, difficult, exciting,
expensive, great, hard, important,
interesting, nice, (im)possible, right,
safe, silly, simple, wrong.*

B Compare this example with the
pattern in A.
  The question is easy to answer.
Here we understand *the question* as the
object of *to answer*. Fewer adjectives can
be used in this pattern than in A. They
include *difficult, expensive,* and *safe.*

We can use *impossible* but not *possible.*
  *The puzzle is **impossible to solve**.*
  (NOT *The puzzle is possible to solve.*)
With *possible* we use pattern A.
  ***It is possible** to solve the puzzle.*

There is no object after the to-infinitive.
  NOT *The question is easy to answer it.*

C The to-infinitive can come after an
adjective + noun.
  *It's an **easy** question **to answer**.*
We can use most of the adjectives in A.

138

D We can use *too* or *enough* in patterns A
and B with many different adjectives.
   *It's **too expensive to take** a taxi.*
   *The streets aren't **safe enough to walk**
   along at night.*

We can use *too* and *enough* in pattern C.
   *It was **too good an** opportunity **to miss.***
   *It's **a big enough** vehicle **to carry** seven.*
   A/an comes after *too* + adjective.

E In the following examples the subject
(*I, we*) is a person.
   *I am **happy to answer** the question.*
   *We were **sorry to hear** your bad news.*
   We can use many different adjectives,
   e.g. *afraid, delighted, eager, glad, lucky,
   proud, ready, surprised, willing.*

F In the following pattern the adjective
expresses a degree of probability.
   *The trial is **likely to last** several weeks.*
   *The party is **sure to be** a success.*
   We can use *bound, certain, due, liable,*
   and *(un)likely.*

TIP

We can use an adjective + to-infinitive
in a number of polite expressions, e.g.
*Pleased to meet you. It was good to
see you. I'll be happy to help. I'd be
delighted to come.*

70 More patterns with the to-infinitive

A *The need to answer*

We can use a to-infinitive after certain verbs and adjectives.

*I **need to answer** these emails.*
*Laura is **reluctant to take** part.*

We can also use a to-infinitive after related nouns. As well as *I need to answer*, we can say *the **need to answer**.*

*There's no **need to answer** all of them.*
*I understand her **reluctance to take** part.*

Nouns that we can use in this pattern include: *ability, anxiety, attempt, choice, decision, demand, desire, determination, failure, intention, offer, plan, promise, proposal, refusal, request, threat, willingness, wish.*

Other nouns which can take a to-infinitive include: *chance, effort, idea, opportunity, power, race, reason, time, way.*

*You'll have a **chance to ask** questions.*

B *A question to answer*

In this pattern the to-infinitive expresses necessity or possibility.

*You've got some **questions to answer**.*
(questions that you **have to** answer)
*Take **something to read** on the train.*
(something that you **can** read)

C *What to do*

We can use a question word or phrase before a to-infinitive.

*I just don't know **what to say**.*
*No one told Tom **where to meet** us.*
*I wasn't sure **how much to tip** the waiter.*

The pattern expresses an indirect question about what the best action is. *I don't know what to say* means that I don't know what I **should** say.

We can also use *whether* + to-infinitive.

*I was wondering **whether to ring** you.*
*Paul can't decide **whether to go** or not.*
(He can't decide whether he **should** go.)

After *what, which, whose, how many,* and *how much,* we can use a noun.

*I didn't know **what size to buy**.*
*The driver wasn't sure **which way to go**.*

When we talk about teaching and learning, we can use *learn (how) to, tell/show someone how to,* and *teach someone how to.*

*Students **learn (how) to plan** their work.*
*The instructor **showed us how to give** the kiss of life.*

TIP

Do not use an infinitive after *if*. Say *I don't know whether to accept* but not *~~I don't know if to accept~~*.

For and *of* with a to-infinitive

A We can use a to-infinitive after *for* +
noun phrase.

> *My wish is **for the world to be** at peace.*
> *It's important **for her to train** regularly
> if she wants to compete.*

The noun phrase (*the world, her*) is the
object of *for* and also functions as the
subject of the to-infinitive. A pronoun
has the object form (*her*).

B The for-pattern can begin a sentence.

> ***For a newspaper to publish** such lies is
> absolutely disgraceful.*

But more often we use *it* as the subject.

> ***It** is absolutely disgraceful **for a
> newspaper to publish** such lies.*

C The pattern can express purpose.

> ***For plants to grow** properly, you need
> to water them regularly.*
> *There are telephones **for drivers to call**
> for help if they break down.*

D We can use the pattern after a verb
which combines with *for*.

> *We've arranged **for plans to be drawn**.*
> *It took ages **for everyone to check** in.*
> *I'll wait **for you to finish** your breakfast.*

Such verbs are: *arrange for, ask for,
call for, look for, pay for, send for, take
(time) for, wait for.*

E Many adjectives and nouns which take a to-infinitive can also take the pattern with *for*. For example, we can say that something is *easy to do* or *easy **for someone** to do*.

> It's easy **for people to criticize**.
> There's no need **for you to go**.
> I've brought some photos **for everyone to have** a look at.

F We use *of* + noun phrase + to-infinitive after adjectives that say what people are like or how they behave.

> It was kind **of you to help** me.
> It was rude **of your friend not to shake** hands with anyone.

The adjectives include: *brave, careless, clever, foolish, generous, good, kind, mean, nice, rude, selfish, silly, stupid, typical, unfair, unreasonable, unwise, wrong*.

Some of these adjectives can take the pattern with *for*. Compare these sentences.

> It was nice **of** Tom to walk the dog.
> (It was a kind action by Tom.)
> It was nice **for** Tom to walk the dog.
> (It was a pleasant experience for Tom.)

TIP

You can use *of* in this sense when thanking someone, e.g. *That's very kind of you* or *It was very good of you to help*.

72 The infinitive without *to*

A An infinitive without *to* can have these forms.

- Simple: *do*
- Perfect: *have done*
- Continuous: *be doing*
- Perfect + continuous: *have been doing*

B We use the infinitive without *to* after a modal verb.

> Nothing **will go** wrong.
> You **could have phoned** me.
> I **should be working** really.
> Your friend **must have been joking**.

But note *be able to, be allowed to, be going to, have to,* and *ought to.*

> I **ought to be working** really.

C We use the infinitive without *to* after *had better, would rather,* and *rather than.*

> We**'d better not be** late.
> I**'d rather have stayed** in than gone out.
> They decided to accept the offer **rather than take/taking** their case to court.

D *Make, let,* and *have* can take an object and an infinitive without *to.*

> The official **made me fill** out a form.
> They **let the pupils go** home early.
> I'll **have the porter bring** up your bags.
> (I'll tell the porter to bring up your bags.)

Here are some more examples with *let*.
*I can **let you have** a copy.* (give you)
*Please **let us know**.* (tell us)
***Let me go** or I'll scream.* (release me)

Compare *force*, *allow*, and *get*, which all take a to-infinitive.
*The gunman **forced the pilot to land**.*
*They **allowed the pupils to go** home early.*
*I'll **get the porter to bring** up your bags.*

E *See*, *hear*, etc can take an object and an infinitive without *to*.
*Did you **see the men leave** the building?*
*I **heard someone knock** on the door.*
*We **felt the ground shake**.*
We can also use a participle. ➤ 81
*We **felt the ground shaking**.*

F After *except* and *but* (= except), we normally use an infinitive without *to*.
*In the flat I do everything **except cook**.*
*You've done nothing **but grumble** all day.*

G We sometimes put an infinitive after *be* when explaining what action we mean.
*The only thing I can do is **(to) apologize**.*
The infinitive can be with or without *to*.

TIP

We say *They made me wait* without *to*, but with *make* in the passive we use the to-infinitive: *I was made to wait*.

---

73 The gerund

A These are the forms of the gerund.

- Simple: *doing*
  It was nice **meeting** you.
- Perfect: *having done*
  He gave no sign of **having understood**.
- Simple passive: *being done*
  I was angry at **being teased**.
- Perfect passive: *having been done*
  The cyclist was compensated for **having been injured** in the accident.

There are some spelling rules for the ing-form. ➤ 178

In the negative, *not* comes before the gerund.

It was awful **not hearing** any news.
I regret **not having learned** the language.

B A gerund can be followed by an object or complement and/or by one or more adverbials. The gerund together with such phrases is a gerund clause.

No one likes **cleaning shoes**.
Being a doctor means people always want your advice.
Going on holiday makes me nervous.

Or a gerund clause can be just a gerund on its own.

Do you like **dancing**?

C A gerund clause can have a subject.
It comes before the gerund.

> We rely on **our neighbour watering** the
> plants while we're away.
> I dislike **journalists asking** me questions.

The subject can be possessive. Typical
possessive subjects are *my, your,* etc or
a name + *'s.*

> It's a nuisance **you/your coming** in late.
> Do you mind **me/my sitting** here?
> I'm fed up with **Sarah/Sarah's**
> **laughing** at my accent.

Both forms have the same meaning
here. But the possessive is more formal,
and it is less usual in everyday speech.

A possessive is more likely at the
beginning of a sentence.

> **Your coming** in late is a nuisance.
> **Sarah's laughing** at my accent is
> getting on my nerves.

TIP

A gerund is sometimes referred to as
an ing-form. But an ing-form can be
an active participle as well as a gerund.
Gerund: *Jogging isn't my idea of fun.*
Participle: *He was jogging along the
street.*
But remember that it is more important
to use the forms correctly than to worry
about what to call them.

74 Some patterns with the gerund

A As subject and complement

The gerund clause can be the subject.

Digging is hard work.
Choosing the colour won't be easy.

When we use *it* as the subject, the gerund clause comes at or near the end of the sentence.

It won't be easy *choosing the colour*.

The gerund clause can also be a complement after *be*.

My worst fear *is having nowhere to live*.

B *It, there,* and *have*

We often use a gerund after the subject *it* and certain expressions.

It's no *good* / no *use arguing* with me.
It might be *worth taking* the tour.
It was an *experience seeing* a rodeo.
It's a *nuisance being* without electricity.
It's *fun skiing* down a mountain.

We can use a gerund after *there ... problem/difficulty* and *there ... point*.

There won't be any *problem parking*.
There's no *point waiting* any longer.

There is also a pattern with *have* (= experience) and a gerund.

You won't *have* any *problem parking*.
We *had fun skiing* down the mountain.

C Verb + gerund

Some verbs take a gerund.

*These people **keep sending** me emails.*

For a list of these verbs, ➤ 66C.

D Verb + object + gerund

We can use a gerund after a verb + object.

*I can't **imagine people buying** that.*
*The arrangements **involve us giving** two other people a lift.*

The object of the verb (*people, us*) also functions as the subject of the gerund. A pronoun has the object form (*us*).

We can use a possessive form. ➤ 73C

*The arrangements **involve your giving** two other people a lift.*

The verbs we can use before an object + gerund include: *avoid, can't bear, discuss, dislike, enjoy, excuse, experience, (not) forget, forgive, hate, can't help, imagine, involve, justify, mind, miss, prevent, remember, resent, risk, save, can't stand, stop, tolerate, understand.*

TIP

Use a gerund at the start of a sentence or a to-infinitive at the end. Say ***Booking** early was a good idea* or *It was a good idea **to book** early.*

---

75 Preposition + gerund

A We sometimes use a gerund after a preposition.

*I drove all the way **without stopping**.*

We cannot use a to-infinitive or a that-clause here.

NOT ~~I drove all the way without to stop.~~

NOT ~~I drove all the way without I stopped.~~

For the gerund after combinations of verb/adjective/noun + preposition, ➤ 76.

B Here are some more examples.

*I got there **by hitching** a lift.*

***Instead of landing** at Heathrow, we had to go to Manchester.*

*Please turn off the lights **before leaving**.*

***Far from being** the end of the story, it was only the beginning.*

*I feel tired **in spite of having slept** well.*

*The drug was finally approved for sale **after being tested**.*

We can use a gerund after these prepositions: *after, against, as a result of, as for, as well as, because of, before, besides, by, by means of, despite, far from, for, from, how/what about, in, in addition to, in favour of, in spite of, in the process of, instead of, on, on account of, on the point of, since, through, with, without.*

C With most of these prepositions, the gerund can have a subject.

*The picture was hung upside down **without anyone noticing**.*
***Despite me/my reminding** him, he completely forgot.*

D *On* and *in* have special meanings in this pattern.

***On turning** the corner, I saw a most unexpected sight.*
(As soon as I had turned the corner, ...)
***In building** the motorway, they attracted new industry to the area.*
(As a result of building the motorway, ...)
This use of *on* and *in* is a little formal.

E We can use *for* + gerund to explain the use or purpose of something.

*These pages are **for making** notes on.*

F We can also use a gerund after *than*, *as*, and *like* expressing comparison.

*A holiday is nicer **than sitting** at a desk.*
*Walking is good for you, but not as good **as swimming**.*
*Getting information from the company is **like getting** blood out of a stone.*

TIP

You can use *how about* or *what about* + gerund to make a suggestion, e.g. **How about going** to the park?

76 Combination + gerund

A Verb + preposition

We can use a gerund after a prepositional verb such as *think of* or *insist on*.

I'm **thinking of selling** my car.
Paul **insists on getting** there early.
They **apologized for making** a mess.

Other prepositional verbs in this pattern include: *(dis)agree with, (dis)approve of, believe in, care for, complain about, concentrate on, cope with, count on, depend on, dream about/of, feel like, get on with, protest at/about, put up with, refrain from, rely on, succeed in, talk about, vote for, worry about.* For prepositional verbs with *to,* ➤ 77C.

B Verb + object + preposition

We can use a gerund after a verb + object + preposition.

Please **forgive me for interrupting**.
A man **saved the child from drowning**.

Other verbs in this pattern include: *accuse ... of, arrest ... for, blame ... for, congratulate ... on, criticize ... for, discourage ... from, forgive ... for, involve ... in, keep ... from, praise ... for, prevent ... from, punish ... for, remind ... of, stop ... from, suspect ... of, thank ... for, use ... for, warn ... about.*

C Adjective + preposition

A gerund can follow an adjective + preposition.

*Lucy is **keen on riding**.*

*I'm **nervous of saying** the wrong thing.*

Other adjectives include: *afraid of, anxious about, aware of, bad at, bored with, capable of, engaged in, famous for, fed up with, fond of, good at, grateful for, guilty of, (un)happy about, opposed to, pleased about, ready for, responsible for, sorry for, tired of, worried about, wrong with.*

D Noun + preposition

A gerund can follow a noun + preposition.

*What's your **excuse for being** late?*

*It's a **question of getting** organized.*

Of is the most common preposition in this pattern. We can use it with: *aim, chance, danger, effect, experience, fact, fear, habit, hope, idea, importance, intention, job, point, possibility, problem, purpose, risk, way.* Note also *difficulty in, interest in, reason for, success in.*

TIP

A gerund in patterns A, C, and D can have a subject, e.g. *Paul insists on **everyone** getting there early.*
*I'm nervous of **my sister** saying the wrong thing. It's a question of **people** getting organized.*

For doing, to do, to doing

A After some verbs and adjectives we can use either a preposition + gerund or a to-infinitive with no difference in meaning.

*The people **voted for joining** / **to join** the European Community.*

Other examples are: *aim at doing / to do, annoyed at finding / to find, content with being / to be, excited at seeing / to see, grateful for having / to have, surprised at finding / to find.*

B Sometimes there are two different patterns with different uses. Compare the examples.

*I don't **agree with dumping** waste in the sea.* (I don't think it is right.)

*We all **agreed to meet** the next day.* (We decided to meet.)

*This **reminds me of walking** in Scotland years ago.* (*this* = impersonal subject)

*Why didn't you **remind me to bring** a map?* (*you* = personal subject)

*Karen was **pleased about winning** / **to win** a prize.* (pleased about a past event)

*I'm **pleased to meet** you.* (in the present)

*He's **afraid of being hit** by a car.* (He is afraid because he might be hit.)

*He is **afraid to cross** / **afraid of crossing** the road.* (He won't cross because he is afraid.)

154

I'm **ashamed of making** mistakes. (I'm
ashamed because I make mistakes.)
I'm **ashamed to speak**. (I won't speak
because it makes me ashamed.)
Jane was **anxious about losing** the way.
(She was worried.)
Jane was **anxious to get** home. (She
wanted to get home.)
I'm **sorry for making / to have made**
such a fuss. (an apology for a past action)
Sorry to disturb / for disturbing you.
(an apology for an action now)

C *To* can be a preposition, or part of a
to-infinitive.
I don't object **to paying** something.
I expect **to pay** the minimum amount.

After the preposition *to*, we can use a
noun clause.
I don't object **to the suggestion**.
We cannot do this with a to-infinitive.

We can use a gerund (not an infinitive)
after: *admit to, close to, confess to,
look forward to, object to, objection to,
opposed to, resigned to, resort to, be
used to* ➤ 58B.

TIP

When you arrange to see someone that
you haven't seen for a while, it is polite
to say *I look forward to seeing you*
(not ~~I look forward to see you~~).

---

8 Determiner + gerund

A We can sometimes put a determiner such as *the* before a gerund.
*Nancy likes her new job, but **the driving** makes her tired.*

Compare the two sentences.
***Driving** makes her tired.*
(all driving, driving in general)
***The driving** makes her tired.*
(the driving she does in her job)
The + gerund is specific rather than general.

We use *do the* + gerund for some types of work, especially routine housework.
*I usually **do the cleaning** at weekends.*
*Someone **does the gardening** for us.*

B As well as *the*, we can use *this*, *that*, *some*, *no*, *a lot of*, *a little*, *a bit of*, and *much*.
***This arguing** gets on my nerves.*
*I might do **some fishing** at the weekend.*
***No parking**. (Parking is not allowed.)*
*I'd better do **a bit of tidying** up.*
*Luckily there isn't **much ironing** to do.*

We can also use a possessive.
***Your driving** terrifies me.*
(the way you drive)
Compare the subject *your*. ► 73C
***Your driving** isn't advisable. You're tired.*
(the idea of you driving)

C The gerund cannot be plural.
NOT *Your drivings terrify me.*
But there are some words formed from
verb + *-ing* which are ordinary nouns
and can be plural.
*I have to attend lots of **meetings**.*
*We were surrounded by tall **buildings**.*

D A gerund clause can have an object.
*Our main job is **keeping records**.*
***Playing ball games** is prohibited.*

Sometimes we can use the pattern *the*
+ gerund + *of* + object.
*Our main job is **the keeping of records**.*
***The playing of ball games** is prohibited.*
This pattern with *of* can be rather
formal and is typical of an official,
written style.

Sometimes the noun phrase after *of* is
the understood subject.
*I was suddenly woken by **the ringing of**
the telephone.*
(The phone was ringing.)

TIP

In the of-pattern we often use other
abstract nouns rather than a gerund.
For example, *the management of
the economy* is more usual than *the
managing of the economy*, and *the
education of children* more usual than
the educating of children.

---

79 Participles

A There are three main participle forms.
An **active** participle is a verb + *-ing*,
sometimes called a 'present participle'.
*I fell asleep **watching** television.*
For spelling rules, ➤ 178.

The **past** participle has a regular
ending in *-ed*. For spelling rules,
➤ 177B, 178B.
*I've **watched** all these DVDs.*
For irregular forms, ➤ page 362.
*The journey has **taken** a long time.*

The **passive** participle has the same
form as the past participle.
*The game was **watched** by a few people.*
***Taken** by surprise, he just stood there.*

We can put *not* before a participle.
*I sat there **not listening** to a word.*

B The participles combine with *be* or
have in the following verb forms.
* Continuous: *be* + active participle
  *The train **was stopping**.*
* Perfect: *have* + past participle
  *My watch **has stopped**.*
* Passive: *be* + passive participle
  *We **were stopped** by the police.*

On the following pages, other uses of
the participles are dealt with.

C As well as the main participles, there are three more complex forms.

- Perfect participle: *having* + past participle

  Having cooked *the meal, they ate.*
- Perfect passive participle: *having been* + passive participle

  *The meal **having been cooked**, they ate.*
- Continuous passive participle: *being* + passive participle

  *The watched the meal **being cooked**.*

D A participle can be followed by an object or complement and/or by one or more adverbials in a participle clause.

  *We saw a policeman **chasing someone**.*
  ***Injured in the leg**, he left the field.*

Or the clause can be just a participle.

  *I just lay there **thinking**.*

E A participle clause can sometimes have a subject.

  ***The flat being untidy**, I had to clear up.*
  ***The lights having fused**, it was dark.*

TIP

Try to avoid writing sentences like this: ~~Walking along the street, a car raced past~~. This 'hanging participle' (*walking*) makes it sound as if the car was walking, which is nonsense. The subject of the main clause should be the people walking. Write: ***Walking*** *along the street,* ***we*** *saw a car race past.*

---

88 Participle + noun

A We can use an active or passive
participle before a noun.
Cheering crowds *welcomed the team.*
(crowds who were cheering)
Boiling water *turns to steam.*
(water which is boiling)
The *damaged goods* *were unusable.*
(goods which had been damaged)
The terrorists used a *stolen car.*
(a car which had been stolen)
The participle functions like an
adjective. Compare *cheering* crowds /
noisy crowds and *boiling* water / *hot*
water.

B Sometimes we use a participle with a
prefix (e.g. *re-*, *mis-*).
a rewritten version   a misspent youth
underfed children   an unsmiling face
a disconnected telephone

C There are a few past participles that we
can use before a noun.
The road is blocked by a fallen tree.
(a tree which has fallen)

Compare the participles.
The escaped prisoner was recaptured.
(Past: he had escaped)
The injured prisoner saw a doctor.
(Passive: he had been injured)

D Sometimes we put an adverb before the participle.

fanatically cheering crowds
properly trained staff

We can also form a compound participle.

a ***fast-growing*** economy
earth-moving equipment
a ***nice-looking*** jacket
oil-fired central heating

We do not use longer phrases before the participle.

NOT ~~written in pencil notes~~
NOT ~~with great enthusiasm cheering crowds~~

But we can say *notes written in pencil*.

➤ 176

E We can add *-ed* to some nouns.

a ***walled*** city (a city with a wall)

This happens mostly with compounds.

a ***dark-haired*** man
(a man with dark hair)
a ***short-sleeved*** shirt
(a shirt with short sleeves)

TIP

It is neater to say *a stolen car* than *a car which has been stolen*. But not all combinations are possible. We can say *a barking dog* but not ~~an eating dog~~. So it is safer to use only those combinations that you have already heard or seen, such as *boiling water*.

---

81 Verb + object + participle

A *I saw you doing it*

We can use an object + active participle after a verb of perception, e.g. *see.*

I saw two men cutting down a tree.

We heard you arguing with Steven.

We can use: *feel, hear, listen to, notice, observe, see, smell, watch.*

B *I saw you do/doing it*

There is also a pattern with object + infinitive without *to.* We use it to refer to a complete action.

I saw them cut the tree down. It didn't take long. (I saw them. They cut it down.)

The participle means that the action was in progress at the time.

I saw them cutting the tree down as I went past. (I saw them. They were cutting it down.)

When we talk about a short action, we can use either form.

We didn't notice anyone leave/leaving the building.

C *I saw it (being) done*

The patterns in B can be used with a participle in the passive.

I saw it cut down. (complete action)

I saw it being cut down. (in progress)

We heard a shot fired. (complete action)

We heard shots being fired. (in progress)

D *I kept you waiting*

We can use an object + participle after:
catch, find, get, have, keep, leave, start.

> They **caught a student cheating**.
> I **got the printer working** again.
> The trainer **had the players running**
> around the field. (He made them run.)

We can also use *spend, waste,* or *lose*
and an amount of time or money.

> I've **spent an hour looking** for that disk.
> He **wasted money betting** on horses.

We can use a passive participle with
find, get, have, and *leave.*

> The police **found a body buried** nearby.

E *You were seen doing it*

Some verbs in A and D can be passive
before the participle: *hear, observe, see,
catch, find, keep, leave.*

> The men **were seen cutting** down a tree.
> A student **was caught cheating**.

F *I want it done*

A passive participle (or to-infinitive) is
used after *hate, like, love, need, prefer,*
and *want.*

> I **want this page (to be) copied**, please.
> We **prefer the sound (to be) turned** off.

TIP

Two useful sentences are an apology,
Sorry to keep you waiting, and a warning,
I can smell something burning.

82 Participles for time and reason

A Time

A clause of time can have an active participle.

> *Mike hurt his hand **playing volleyball**.*
> *I was rushing around **serving tea**.*

The actions take place at the same time.

The participle can come first in writing.

> ***Coming up the steps**, I slipped and fell.*

We can also use a participle for two short connected actions, one after the other.

> ***Opening the file**, he took out a photo.*

This pattern is rather literary.

When a short action comes before another connected one, we can use a perfect participle for the first action.

> ***Having opened** the file, / **Opening** the file, he took out a photo.*

When the first action is not short, we must use the perfect.

> ***Having studied** the photo, he replaced it.*
> ***Having dug** a hole, the men went away.*
> (NOT ~~*Digging a hole, the men went away.*~~)

The passive participle can be simple, continuous, or perfect.

> *He walked slowly, **helped by a nurse**.*
> *I can't stay here **being bitten** by insects.*
> *A hole **having been dug**, they went away.*

B Reason

A participle clause can express reason.

Being rather busy, I forgot the time.

Not feeling well, Emma went to lie down.

Having lost my passport, I have to apply for a new one.

The restaurant having closed, there was nowhere to eat.

This type of participle clause can be rather formal.

We can use *with* before a participle clause with a subject.

I can't concentrate *with you talking*.

With the restaurant having closed, there was nowhere to eat.

This pattern is neutral in style and less formal than *The restaurant having closed* ...

The passive participle can be simple, continuous, or perfect.

He died young, *killed in a road accident*.

The ponies get fat, *being fed by tourists*.

Having been renovated at great expense, the palace looks magnificent.

TIP

Some of these patterns are a little tricky and can sound formal. It is usually safer to use conjunctions such as *when*, *while*, and *because* to make your meaning clear.

83 Some patterns with participles

A *I sat reading*

We can use a participle after *go*, *lie*, *run*, *sit*, and *stand*.

Everyone **stood watching** the aircraft.
The girl **lay trapped** in the wreckage.

B *I went swimming*

We use *go* + active participle for leisure activities that we go out to do.

We **went riding** yesterday.
Simon has **gone fishing**.

C Conjunction + participle

We can use an active or passive participle after some conjunctions.

Wear gloves **when using** an electric saw.
Once opened, the contents should be consumed within three days.

The pattern is used mainly in writing and with *although*, *if*, *once*, *unless*, *until*, *when*, *whenever*, and *while*.

D Result

A clause with an active participle can express result.

The film star made a dramatic entrance, **attracting everyone's attention**.
They pumped waste into the river, **killing all the fish**. (... and killed all the fish.)

E Conditions

A participle clause can express a condition.

*We'll eat outside, **weather permitting**.*
(if the weather permits it)
***Taken daily**, vitamin pills can improve your health.* (if they are taken daily)

F *With* for details

This example has *with* and a subject of the participle clause.

*There were scenes of celebration, **with people dancing** in the streets.*

The clause adds detail.

G *Following, considering*, etc

Some participles are used as prepositions.

***Following** the reception, there will be a talk by the professor.* (after the reception)
***Considering** the weather, the day was a great success.* (in view of the weather)
*I am writing **regarding** your complaint.*
(about your complaint)

H Idioms

Some participle clauses are idioms.

***Strictly speaking**, that's not allowed.*
***All being well**, we'll be there by six.*

TIP

Use *talking of* to link to a new topic, e.g.
*I'm doing a computer course. ~ **Talking of** computers, ours are all down.*

---

84 Nouns and noun phrases

A A noun is a word like *car*, *uncle*, or *success*. Nouns have different kinds of meaning. There are:

- concrete nouns, e.g. *computer*, *dog*
- abstract nouns, e.g. *strength*, *excitement*
- nouns referring to events, e.g. *festival*
- nouns referring to roles, e.g. *designer*
- names, e.g. *America*

B Some nouns have a plural form with *s*, e.g. *cars*, *dogs*. There are also irregular plurals, e.g. *feet*, *knives*. ➤ 85C

The only other ending that we put on a noun is the possessive form with *'s* or *s'*, e.g. *the driver's seat*. ➤ 86

C A noun phrase can be a noun on its own. *We all need **money**. **Silence** is golden.*

But more often a noun combines with other words to form a noun phrase. *some money   the road   his opinion several of the young people*

D A noun phrase can be the subject, object, or complement of a sentence. ***The vehicle** hit **a tree**. **The day** was **an absolute disaster**.* It can also come after a preposition. *We were all looking **at the photos**.*

E These words can combine with a noun to form a noun phrase.

- Articles, e.g. *a house*, *the police* ➤ 95
- Possessives, e.g. *my job* ➤ 102
- Demonstratives, e.g. *this way* ➤ 103
- Quantifiers, e.g. *many cars*, *ten days* ➤ 104
- Adjectives, e.g. *a good idea* ➤ 115
- Other nouns, e.g. *a car accident* ➤ 91

F We can use a phrase after a noun to modify it. The phrase can be one of these types.

- Prepositional phrase, e.g. *tea for two*
- Adverb phrase, e.g. *the people upstairs*
- Adjective phrase, e.g. *a hole full of water*
- Noun phrase, e.g. *the weather that day*

The prepositional phrase is the most common.

> *I'd love an apartment on Fifth Avenue.*
> *The period after lunch is always quiet.*

We can use two or more phrases, or phrases and clauses together.

> *Passengers on services through the tunnel will suffer delays.*
> *Police are baffled by the case of a girl from Coventry who has disappeared.*

TIP

For noun + preposition combinations, e.g. *the idea of*, *the reason for*, ➤ 147D.

---

85 The plural of nouns

A Regular plurals

A countable noun can be singular or
plural. The regular plural ending is -s
or -es.

one book → *two books*
one dish → *two dishes*.

We add -es after a sound like *s*, *z*, *sh*,
or *ch*. For pronunciation and spelling,
➤ 177A.

B Compound nouns

To form the plural of a compound
noun or two nouns together, we add
-s/-es.

weekends   fire-fighters   metal boxes

We also add -s to a verb + adverb
compound.

fry-ups   breakdowns   handouts

But when there is a prepositional
phrase, we make the first noun plural.

Doctors-of-Philosophy   mothers-in-law

And with a noun in -er + adverb, we
add -s/-es to the noun.

passers-by   runners-up

C Irregular plurals

Some plurals are formed by changing
the vowel sound.

foot → *feet*   *man* → *men*
mouse → *mice*   *tooth* → *teeth*
woman → *women*

There is an old plural form *-en* which has survived in these two nouns.

child → **children** *ox* → **oxen**

With some nouns we change *f* to *v*.

life → **lives** *half* → **halves**

Others are: *calves, knives, leaves, loaves, shelves, thieves, wives, wolves.* But some nouns ending in *f* or *fe* are regular: *beliefs, chiefs, cliffs, safes.*

In the plural nouns *baths, mouths, paths, truths,* and *youths,* the *ths* sound is usually voiced /ðz/. But *births, deaths,* and *months* are regular /θs/. *Houses* also has two voiced /z/ sounds.

Some nouns have the same singular and plural form. These are *aircraft, spacecraft,* etc, some animals, e.g. *sheep, deer,* and some fish, e.g. *cod.*

A number of words from Greek and Latin have special plural endings. They include: *criterion* → **criteria**, *medium* → **media**, *phenomenon* → **phenomena**, *analysis* → **analyses**, *crisis* → **crises**, *nucleus* → **nuclei**, *stimulus* → **stimuli**.

Other irregular plurals are *penny* → **pence** and *person* → **people**.

TIP

We normally use the plural for a negative or unknown quantity, e.g. *Have you read any good **books** lately?*

86 The possessive form

A Form

Singular noun + *'s*: *my friend's name*
S-plural + *'*: *my friends' names*
Other plurals + *'s*: *the children's names*

We add an apostrophe (') + *s* to a
singular noun; we add an apostrophe
to a plural in *-s*; and we add an
apostrophe + *s* to a plural not ending
in *-s*. For pronunciation, ► 177A.

One, *each other*, and pronouns ending
in *-one/-body* can be possessive.
*I found **someone's** coat here.*

B Use

We use the possessive form for
a connection, often the fact that
someone has something, or something
belongs to them.

Sam's dog   Lucy's idea   people's jobs
Sam's dog means '**the** dog that belongs
to Sam'. So we do not put *the* before a
singular name.

NOT *the Sam's dog*

We can leave out the noun after the
possessive if the meaning is clear.
*Is this your umbrella? ~ No, it's **Peter's**.*

We can sometimes use two possessive
forms together.
*Anita is my **mother's brother's** daughter.*

C Possessive form or *of*?

These two patterns have the same meaning.

Possessive form: *my friend's* name
Of-pattern: *the name of my friend*
Sometimes we can use either form.
But often only one is possible.

> *your dad's* car (NOT ~~the car of your dad~~)
> *the end of the term* (NOT ~~the term's end~~)

We normally use the possessive with people.

> *my uncle's* job   *the Atkinsons' house*

But with a long description, we use *of*.

> It's the home *of a wealthy businessman from Moscow*.

The of-pattern is sometimes possible for relations between people.

> *the girl's* mother / *the mother of the girl*

We generally use *of* with things.

> *the middle of the night*
> *the results of the inquiry*

But we can use both patterns with places or organizations.

> *Scotland's* rivers / *the rivers of Scotland*
> *the firm's* policy / *the policy of the firm*

TIP

Use the possessive form with people and the of-pattern with things. Say *my sister's* address but *the address of the website*.

173

88 Some uses of the possessive

A As well as the idea of belonging (► 86B), the possessive can also mean that something is intended for someone.
a customers' car park (for customers)
a children's playground (for children)

B The possessive can show the type of thing we are talking about.
a bird's nest (a nest made by a bird)
a man's voice (a male voice)

C We can use the possessive for the person doing the action.
The man's reply surprised us.
(The man replied.)

D We can also use the possessive for the person who the action is directed at.
Emma's promotion was well deserved.
(They promoted Emma.)

E In these examples the possessive pattern is used for a person's qualities.
The man's stupidity / The stupidity of the man annoys me. (The man is stupid.)

F The possessive form can express time.
Do we have yesterday's newspaper?
Last month's figures were excellent.
Last month's figures means the figures for last month.

We cannot use a time of day.
   the three o'clock race
   (NOT ~~three o'clock's race~~)

G The possessive form can also express
length of time.
   *The coast is **half an hour's drive** away.*
   *There's **a whole year's work** on this disk.*

We sometimes use a plural noun.
   *I would like **a few minutes' rest**.*
   *We get just **three weeks' holiday** a year.*
The apostrophe goes after the plural *-s*.

H We can use the possessive form
without a following noun for
someone's home or a particular kind
of shop or office.
   *We're all meeting at **Dave's** (house/flat).*
   *Is there a **baker's** (shop) near here, do
   you know?*
   *I was in the waiting room at the
   dentist's.*

We can also use company names.
   *I bought the milk at **Tesco's**.*

TIP

People whose first language is English
are not always consistent in their use
of the apostrophe, and it is sometimes
missed out. Many companies leave out
the apostrophe from their name, e.g.
Barclays Bank.

88 Countable and uncountable nouns

A **Countable** nouns can be singular or plural: *boat(s)*, *day(s)*, *problem(s)*, *man/men*. We use countable nouns for separate, individual things we can count: *a boat*, *three days*, *some problems*, etc. Many countable nouns are concrete, e.g. *car(s)*, *shop(s)*. But some are abstract, e.g. *idea(s)*, *situation(s)*.

Uncountable nouns are neither singular nor plural: *air*, *butter*, *electricity*, *music*, *peace*. We use uncountable nouns for things that do not naturally divide into separate units. Many uncountable nouns are abstract, e.g. *happiness*, *security*. But some are concrete, e.g. *water*, *sand*.

Many nouns can be either countable or uncountable. ➤ 90

B An uncountable noun takes a singular verb, and we use *this/that/it*, not *these/those/they*.
   This milk *is* off. I'll pour *it* away.

We can use an uncountable noun on its own.
   Water is essential for life.
   (NOT ~~The water is essential for life.~~)

But a singular noun normally has to have a word like *a* or *the*.
The boat *leaves at ten o'clock.*
(NOT ~~Boat leaves at ten o'clock.~~)

Some words go with both countable and uncountable nouns: **the** *boat* or **the** *water* and **my** *boat* or **my** *water*. But some words go with only one kind of noun: **a** *boat* but not ~~a water~~ and how **many** *boats* but how **much** *water*.

C   We cannot say ~~a flour~~ or ~~two woods~~. If we want to say how much flour or wood, then we use a pattern with *of*.
a packet of flour   **two pieces of wood**
We cannot leave out *of*.

We can also use *of* before a plural noun.
a box of matches   **a kilo of tomatoes**

Before *of* + uncountable or plural noun we can use containers or measurements.
a cup of *coffee*   **a bottle of** *wine*
three **metres of** *material*
Before *of* + uncountable noun we can use *piece* and nouns of similar meaning.
a sheet/piece/bit of *paper*
a drop of *water/milk/oil*

TIP

Crowd of, *group of*, and *series of* go with
a plural noun, e.g. *a crowd of people, a
group of tourists, a series of mistakes*,
but not ~~a series of confusion~~.

---

89 *Information, news*, etc

A It is not always clear from the meaning whether a noun is countable or uncountable. For example, *information*, *news*, and *furniture* are uncountable.

> *I've found out **some information**.*
> (NOT *an information*)
> *There **was** no news of the missing child.*
> (NOT *There were no news.*)
> *They had very **little furniture**.*
> (NOT *very few furnitures*)

But we can often use *piece/bit/item of* with such nouns.

> *I've found out **a piece of information**.*
> *They had very **few items of furniture**.*

B Here are some more uncountable nouns (in **bold type**) whose equivalents may be countable in other languages. Some countable expressions are given in brackets.

> *looking for **accommodation** (but a place to live)*
> *getting some **advice***
> *taking some **baggage/luggage** (but some bags/cases)*
> *paying in **cash** (but notes and coins)*
> *some warm **clothing** (but some warm jumpers)*
> *in lovely **country/countryside/scenery***
> *doing **damage/harm** to the environment*

*speaking good **English***
*needing some **equipment***
*finding some **evidence***
*having some **fun** (but a good time)*
*enjoying good **health***
*doing **homework** (but a task / a project)*
*doing **housework** (but doing chores)*
*buying some **jewellery***
*owner of some **land***
*a little **leisure***
***lightning** in the sky*
*dropping some **litter/rubbish***
*enjoying good **luck***
*installing **machinery** (but a machine)*
*leaving without **permission***
*causing **pollution***
*making some **progress***
*lots of **publicity** (but lots of adverts)*
*having some **rain***
*doing **research***
*loading my **stuff** in the car (but my things)*
*hearing **thunder***
*a queue of **traffic** (but cars/vehicles)*
*work involving **travel** (but journeys/trips)*
*having nice **weather***
*doing some **work** (but a job)*

TIP

When you see or hear the pattern with *of*, try to learn the phrase as a whole: *a piece of equipment, a bit of rubbish, a shower of rain, a stroke of luck, a flash of lightning, a clap of thunder.*

90 Nouns either countable or uncountable

A Some nouns are countable when they mean something separate and individual but uncountable when they mean a material or substance.

Countable:

*They had **a** red **carpet** in the living room.*
*The mob threw **stones** at the police.*

Uncountable:

*We bought ten square metres of **carpet**.*
*The palace was rebuilt in **stone**.*

B Animals, vegetables, and fruit are uncountable when we cut or divide them.

Countable:

*I picked **some tomatoes**.*

Uncountable:

*I ordered a pizza with **tomato**.*

C Feelings are usually uncountable.

*The animal was trembling with **fear**.*

But some can be countable, especially for a feeling about something specific.

***a fear** of dogs **our hopes** for the future*

D Some abstract nouns can be either.

*Do we have **a choice** / **any choice**?*
*We have received **some criticism(s)**.*

Others include: *advantage, chance, change, detail, difference, difficulty, effect, effort, idea, impact, point, reason, response.*

E Often the countable noun means a specific example, and the uncountable noun has a more general meaning.

Countable

I'm running **a** small **business.** (a company)
I had **a conversation** with your friend.
I've bought a **drawing** / a **painting.** (a picture)
We had **an** interesting **experience** yesterday.
I'll have **a glass** of water.
There's **a hair** on your sweater.
I need **an iron.** (for pressing clothes)
He led **an** interesting **life.**
I just heard **a noise.**
We usually buy a daily **paper.** (newspaper)
Is chess a game or **a sport?**
I've been here lots of **times** before. (occasions)
It was a long and bloody **war.**

Uncountable

Business is booming. (economic activity)
They say the art of **conversation** is dying.
I'm no good at **drawing/painting.** (the activity)
He hasn't had very much **experience** in the job.
You should wear gloves when handling **glass.**
When did you last comb your **hair?**
These tablets contain **iron.** (a metal)
Life just isn't fair, is it?
Constant **noise** can cause stress.
Have we got **any** wrapping **paper?**
There's always **sport** on television.
I'm busy. I haven't got **much time.**
I've always been against **war** on principle.

91 Two nouns together

A We often use one noun before another.
The first noun modifies the second
– tells us what kind it is or what it is for.
vitamin pills (pills containing vitamins)
a phone bill (a bill for using the phone)
a rail link (a link by rail)

B Some combinations are written as
two separate words, e.g. *address book*,
paper cup, and some are written as one
word, e.g. *armchair*, *bookshop*. Some
combinations may have a hyphen,
though this is old-fashioned.

C The first noun is usually singular, even
if it refers to more than one.
*a **vegetable** garden   a **picture** gallery*
A *picture gallery* contains **pictures**.

But there are some exceptions.
***careers** information   a **sports** shop*

D We can use more than two nouns
together.
credit card charges
a motorway service station
an air accident investigation team

E The first noun can express purpose.
hand cream (cream for your hands)
a car park   a coffee table

It can also express means.
a car journey (a journey by car)
a fax message   an oil lamp

The first noun can say what the topic is.
a war film (a film about war)
a crime story   a computer magazine

Here the first noun is the object of an action done by a person or a machine.
a taxi driver (a person who drives a taxi)
a chess player   a food mixer
a lawnmower   steel production

The first noun can express time or place.
a summer holiday (a holiday in summer)
a country pub (a pub in the country)
a future date   breakfast television
a motorway bridge   a London suburb

It can be a kind of material.
a plastic bag (a bag made of plastic)
a brick wall   a cardboard box

The pattern can express the idea that something is a part of something else.
the car door (the door of the car)
the TV screen   the town centre

TIP

A *milk bottle* is a bottle for putting milk in, e.g. *an empty milk bottle*. A *bottle of milk* is a bottle full of milk, e.g. *a bottle of milk in the fridge*.

92 Agreement

A 'Agreement' means using a singular
verb after a singular or uncountable
subject and a plural verb after a plural
subject.

Singular: *The **house is** empty.*
              *This **coat looks** nice.*
Plural: *The **houses are** empty.*
              *These **coats look** nice.*

This happens when we use a present-
tense verb in the third person.

With a past-tense verb, there is
agreement only with *be*.

Singular: *The **house was** empty.*
Plural: *The **houses were** empty.*

Other verbs have only one form.
    *The house/houses **looked** empty.*

B Phrases linked by *and* take a plural verb.
    ***Simon and Chloe go** sailing.*
    ***Wheat and maize are** exported.*
But two things seen as a single idea
take a singular verb.
    ***Bread and butter was** all we had.*

Two references to the same thing do
not make a subject plural.
    ***Simon**, my neighbour, **goes** sailing.*

C When two singular phrases are linked
by *or*, the verb is singular.
    *Either **Thursday or Friday is** OK by me.*

D A phrase of measurement usually takes a singular verb.

Ten miles is *too far to walk.*

E We also use a singular verb after:

- titles and names of one thing

    'Star Wars' was *a very successful film.*
    The United States is *against the plan.*

- a phrase or clause

    Opening our presents was *exciting.*

- a subject with *every* or *each*

    Every/Each pupil has *to take the test.*

- compounds with *every, some, any, no*

    Everyone has *to take the test.*
    Nothing *ever* **happens** *in this place.*

- *who* or *what* as subject

    Who wants *coffee?* ~ *We all do.*

F *Lot/number/couple/majority of* + plural noun usually has a plural verb.

A lot/number of **people have** *complained.*

But *the number of* ... takes a plural verb.

The **number** *of complaints* **is** *increasing.*

G *None/neither/either* and a plural noun can be either singular or plural.

None *(of the pupils)* **has/have** *failed.*
Neither *(of the answers)* **is/are** *correct.*

TIP

After a fraction or percentage, the verb agrees with the noun, e.g. *Two thirds (of the* **drink***) is water. Half the* **birds** **were** *killed.*

---

93 Nouns with a plural form

A Plural noun and plural verb

Some nouns are always plural.

> The **goods were** never delivered.
> (NOT ~~The good was never delivered.~~)

Nouns of this kind include: *belongings, clothes, congratulations, earnings, goods, odds* (probability), *outskirts* (outer parts of a town), *particulars* (details), *premises* (building), *remains* (what is left), *surroundings, thanks, troops.*

Some nouns have a plural-only form which has a different meaning from the singular or uncountable form.

Plural only:

> to carry **arms** (weapons)
> the **contents** of the bag (what is in it)
> go through **customs** at the airport
> pay **damages** of £10,000
> his good **looks** (appearance)
> **regards** to Kate (good wishes)
> my life **savings** (money saved)

Other meanings:

> I hurt my **arm** (part of the body)
> the **content** of the mail (what it says)
> an old **custom** (tradition)
> did some **damage** (e.g. in an accident)
> he gave me a **look** (he looked at me)
> a high **regard** for her (a good opinion)
> a **saving** of £10 (paying less)

B Plural noun form but singular verb

Some nouns end in *-s* but normally take a singular verb.

> The **news isn't** very good, I'm afraid.
> **Maths was** my best subject at school.

Nouns of this kind include *news*; some words for sports and games, e.g. *athletics*, *billiards*, *gymnastics*; some subjects of study, e.g. *maths*, *politics*, *statistics*; and some illnesses, e.g. *measles*, *diabetes*.

C Nouns ending in *-s* in both singular and plural

A few nouns end in *-s* and can be either singular or plural.

> The new comedy **series has** been a flop.
> Bird **species are** numerous in the area.

Some nouns of this kind are *barracks* (a building where soldiers live), *crossroads*, *headquarters*, *means*, *series*, *species*, and *works* (factory).

Barracks, *headquarters*, and *works* can take a plural verb even for a single entity.

> The **headquarters was/were** in Tokyo.

TIP

Politics and *statistics* as subjects take a singular verb, but when they have a more specific meaning, they take a plural, e.g. *His **politics are** very left-wing. The **statistics are** on the Internet.*

94 Pair nouns and group nouns

A Pair nouns

We use a pair noun for certain things made of two similar parts. Most refer to devices, e.g. *scissors, glasses, spectacles, binoculars, scales*, or to clothes that cover part or all of your legs, e.g. *trousers, jeans, shorts, tights, pants*. Note also *pyjamas*.

A pair noun is plural and takes a plural verb.

> ***These trousers need** cleaning.*
> *I need my **glasses**, but I can't find **them**.*
> *There **are some scissors** in the drawer.*

We cannot use *a* or numbers.
(NOT ~~a scissor~~ AND NOT ~~two scissors~~)

We can use *pair of* or *pairs of*.

> *This **pair of trousers** needs cleaning.*
> *Have you got a **pair of binoculars**?*
> *There are three **pairs of scissors** here.*

We have to use *pair* to say how many.

We can also use *pair* with two separate items, e.g. *socks, shoes, boots, gloves*.

> *I've packed six **pairs of socks**.*

B Group nouns

A group noun (or 'collective noun') refers to a group of people, e.g. *audience, club, committee, company, family, government, group, population, press, public, school*.

After a singular group noun, the verb
is usually singular, but it can be plural.
  *The crowd **was**/were in a cheerful mood.*

We use the singular to talk about the
group as a whole: its size or make-up
or how it compares with others.
  *The **class consists** of thirty 11-year-olds.*
  *The **orchestra is** the best in the country.*
A plural is more likely with the
thoughts and feelings of individuals.
  *The **class don't**/doesn't know very much.*
  *The **orchestra are**/is happy to play.*

We normally use *it, its,* and *which/that*
with a singular verb and *they, their,*
and *who/that* with a plural verb.
  *The team **which** lost **was** doing **its** best.*
  *The team **who** lost **were** doing **their** best.*

The names of companies and sports
teams are mostly group nouns.
  ***Tesco sells**/sell organic bananas.*
  ***England has**/have lost again.*

Cattle, livestock, people, police, and
staff are plural.
  *The **police are** questioning a man.*

TIP

The safest choice is the singular verb
because it is more common than the
plural verb, especially in American
English.

---

95 Introduction to *a/an* and *the*

A *A* or *an* is the indefinite article, and *the* is the definite article.

> Storms battered **the** coast of Britain yesterday. **A** man drowned when he was swept into **the** sea by **an** enormous wave during **a** storm at Clacton-on-Sea. Some onlookers tried to rescue **the** man but without success.

We use *a/an* only with a singular noun (*a man, an enormous wave*). The plural/uncountable equivalent is *some* (*some onlookers, some water*), or no article (*storms, water*). We can use *the* with all types of noun.

We use *the* when it is clear which one we mean. We say **the** coast of Britain because there is only one coast of Britain. We say **a** man when we mention him for the first time, but after that we say **the** man, meaning 'the man already mentioned'.

For more details about use, ➤ 96–97.

B Before a consonant sound the articles are *a* and *the*. *A* is pronounced as in the first syllable of *away* and *the* as in *brother*.

> *a book   a ship   a lovely evening*
> pronounced /ə/
> *the book   the ship   the lovely evening*
> pronounced /ðə/

Before a vowel sound the articles are
an and *the*. *An* is pronounced as in
spok**en** and *the* as in wor**thy** (with the
y sound of hap**py**).

> *an apple   an idea   an old picture*
> pronounced /ən/
> *the apple   the idea   the old picture*
> pronounced /ði/

C   *A/an* and *one* both refer to a single
thing, but *one* puts more emphasis on
the number.

> *We have **a** car.* (We can travel by road.)
> *We have **one** car.* (We don't have two.)

We use *one* when we mean a single one
among a larger number.

> ***One** expert says **one** thing, and another
> says something completely different.*
> *Just **one** of the shops was open.*

We use *one* in phrases of time.

> ***One morning** a strange thing happened*
> ***One day** my genius will be recognized.*
> ***At one time** I lived in a caravan.*

TIP

The choice between *a* and *an* depends
on the pronunciation – not the spelling
– of the word after the article. Note
especially words beginning with *o*, *u*, or *h*,
or abbreviations, e.g. ***a** one-day event, **a**
university, **a** European, **a** U-turn, **an** hour,
an MI5 agent.*

---

96 The main uses of *a/an* and *the*

A When something is first mentioned,
the noun usually has *a/an*.
> *A man and a woman were arrested, but
> the woman was later released.*

When it is mentioned again, we use *the*.

Now look at this example.
> *We went by train. The trip took an hour.*

We say *the trip* because the idea of a
trip is mentioned in the first sentence.

B We use *the* for what is unique in the
context.
> *A car stopped and the driver got out.*
> (A car has only one driver.)
> *The sun was still shining.*
> (There is only one in our solar system.)

C We often use *the* when a phrase or
clause follows the noun.
> *Ours is the house on the corner.*

But if the clause or phrase does not
show exactly which one, we use *a/an*.
> *We live in a house by the park.*
> (There are other houses by the park.)

We often use *the* before an of-phrase.
> *They heard the sound of an aircraft.*

D We can use a phrase with *a/an* as
complement to describe something.
> *Yesterday was a beautiful day.*

E We can use a phrase with *a/an* to classify.
  *What kind of bird is that? ~ **A blackbird**.*
  *Anglesey is **an island** off the Welsh coast.*

F We normally use *the* rather than
  a/an with superlative adjectives and
  with *first, last, next, only, right, same,*
  and *wrong.*
  *This is **the tallest building** in the city.*
  *Is this **the first time** you've been here?*
  *I think you went **the wrong way** there.*

G In a generalization, we often use a
  plural or uncountable noun without
  an article.
  *I hate **hospitals**.*
  ***Time** costs **money**, you know.*
  ***Blackbirds** have a lovely song.*
  Here blackbirds means 'all blackbirds'.

  We can use *a/an* in a generalization.
  ***A computer** does what you tell it to do.*
  ***A blackbird** has a lovely song.*
  Here *a blackbird* means 'any blackbird'.

  We can use *the* + singular noun to
  generalize in some contexts.
  ***The blackbird** has a lovely song.*
  ***The customer** is always right.*

TIP

We use *a/an* to classify people by job,
e.g. *My sister is a doctor*, not ~~My sister
is doctor~~.

193

97 Special uses of *a/an* and *the*

A We go to **the** cinema/theatre even if we
do not mean a specific one.
*We haven't been to **the cinema** for ages.*

Look at these examples with *television*
and *radio* in a general sense as a medium.
*My friend has got a job in **television**.*
*We watch **television** in the evenings.*
*We sometimes listen to **the radio**.*
*What's on **television** / on **the radio**?*
On the television is also possible.

With the physical objects, we use *a/an*
or *the* in the usual way.
*There was **a TV** / **a radio** on the shelf.*
*I turned on **the television** / **the radio**.*

We say *the press* (newspapers) and *the
media* (TV, radio, newspapers, etc).
***The media** love a nice scandal.*

B With musical instruments we usually
use *the* for a general ability to play.
*Can you play **the piano**?*

With sports/games we do not use *the*.
*Do you play **tennis** at school?*
*We do **judo** on Saturdays.*

C We use *the bus / the train* for a means
of transport.
*I usually go to work on **the bus**.*
But we say *by bus / by train.* ➤ 142E

D *Town, country, countryside, sea,* and *seaside* usually have *the* in a general meaning.

> *Do you live in **the town** or **the country**?*
> *I'd love a day at **the seaside**.*

We do not mean a specific seaside place.

These examples refer to specific places.

> *In the valley there's **a small town**.*
> *We want to see the sights of **the town**.*
> ***The countryside** here is beautiful.*

The countryside means the scenery in a specific country area.

E We can use *a/an* in expressions of frequency, price, and speed.

> *We walk the dogs **twice a day**.*
> *The material cost **ten pounds a metre**.*
> *The speed limit on motorways is **seventy miles an hour**.*

F We can use *by the* to say how something is measured.

> *Boats can be hired **by the hour**.*
> *Carpets are sold **by the square metre**.*

TIP

We usually say *the police*, e.g. *The police arrived in five minutes.* But we can say *a police officer, the policeman*, etc.

---

98 *A/an*, *some*, *the*, and a noun on its own

A We use *a/an* only with a singular noun. With a plural or uncountable noun we use *some*.

> There's **a rat** in the cellar.
> There are **some rats** in the cellar.
> There's **some milk** in the fridge.

A rat means one rat, *some rats* means a number of rats, and *some milk* means an amount of milk.

We can sometimes leave out *some*.

> There are **rats** in the cellar.
> There's **milk** in the fridge.

B We do not use *some* to classify or describe.

> Those are **rats**, not mice.
> Is this **milk** or cream?
> They're huge **rats**.
> It's fresh **milk**.

C We can use an uncountable or plural noun on its own to make a generalization.

> **Sugar** is bad for your teeth.
> **Life** isn't fair, is it?
> **Children** can be cruel sometimes.

When the meaning is more specific, we use *the*.

> Could you pass **the sugar**, please?
> **The life** of a hill farmer isn't easy.
> **The children** are playing in the garden.

We also often use *the* when there is a phrase after the noun which makes the meaning more specific. We say *Life ...* (in general) but *The life of ...* (a specific person or group of people).

D Compare these patterns.
  *a book on **Irish history***
  *a book on **the history of Ireland***
  *studying **American literature***
  *studying **the literature of America***
We can use an adjective + noun without *the*, or *the* + noun with an of-phrase.

The same thing happens with a noun modifier or a possessive form.
  town planning / the planning of towns
  Mozart's music / the music of Mozart

E Before a noun + of-phrase we usually use *the*.
  ***The safety of passengers** is our priority.*
But with other prepositions, we can use a noun on its own if the meaning is general.
  ***Safety on the railways** is our priority.*
  ***Life in those days** wasn't easy.*

TIP

Many proverbs and sayings begin with an uncountable noun on its own, e.g. ***Life** is sweet. **Money** is the root of all evil. **Love** makes the world go round.*

---

99 A singular noun on its own

Before a singular noun, we normally put a word like *a, the, my*, etc. But there are some exceptions.

A Some nouns can be without *the* when we talk about their normal purpose. These include places of education (*school, college, university*), places of worship (especially *church* and *mosque*), and other public institutions (*prison, jail, court, hospital*).

   __School__ starts at nine o'clock.

   The guilty men were sent to __prison__.

Here *school* means 'school activities' and people are *sent to prison* for their crimes.

But when we talk about a specific building, we use *the*.

   __The school__ is in the centre of the village.
   (the school building)

   Mail is delivered to __the prison__ every day.
   (the prison building)

We use an article if there is a word or phrase modifying the noun.

   They are in __a high-security prison__.

   I'm doing a course at __the new college__.

B *Work, home, town, bed*, and *sea* can also be used without an article.

   I was on my way to __work__.

   We left __home__ at eight o'clock.

Compare these sentences.
*I'm usually in **bed** by eleven.*
***The bed** felt very uncomfortable.*
In bed means 'sleeping/resting in a
bed', but *the bed* means a specific bed.

C We sometimes use no article with
a repeated noun or two nouns in
contrast.
*I lie awake **night** after **night**.*
*It was a fiasco from **start** to **finish**.*

D We often use no article for a unique role
after *elect, appoint, make,* and after *as*.
*The young woman was elected **leader**.*
*As **chairman**, I have to keep order.*
If the role is not unique, use *a/an*.
*As **a member** of the club, I have a vote.*

E With two nouns closely linked, we can
leave out an article to avoid repeating it.
*Put the knife and **fork** on the tray.*
If there is no link, we repeat the article.
*I bought a sweater and **a book**.*

F We also use a singular noun on its own
in some prepositional phrases (e.g. *on
Thursday* ➤ 100, *by train* ➤ 142E) and in
some styles such as instructions ➤ 16F.

TIP

Americans use *the* with hospital and
university. GB: *My sister is **in hospital**.*
US: *My sister is **in the hospital**.*

100

A/an and *the* in phrases of time

A Introduction

In a phrase of time we often use a singular noun without an article.

in winter   on Monday

But we use an article with an adjective or if there is a phrase after the noun.

a cold winter   the Monday before last

See B–H for the various kinds of phrase.

B Years

*in **2004**   from **1939** to **1945***

But: *in **the year** 1066*

C Seasons and months

***Spring** is on the way.*
*It's nice here in (**the**) **summer**.*
*The elections are in **March**.*

But: *a hot **summer**   the **winter** of 2002*

D Special times of the year

*I don't enjoy **Christmas** much.*
*Americans eat turkey at **Thanksgiving**.*

But: *It was **a Christmas** I won't forget.*

E Days of the week

*Our visitors are coming on **Tuesday**.*
But:
*It'll be **the Tuesday** before my holiday.*
*This happened on **a Friday** in July.*
*I'll see you at **the weekend**.*

F Parts of the day and night

> *They reached the camp at **sunset**.*
> *We'll be home before **dark**.*
> But:
> *It was **a wonderful sunset**.*
> *I couldn't see in **the dark**.*

In time phrases we normally use these nouns on their own: *dawn, daybreak, sunrise; midday, noon; dusk, sunset, twilight; dark, nightfall, midnight*. But we use an article for the physical aspect, e.g. not being able to see in *the* dark.

G Meals

> ***Breakfast** is from seven o'clock.*
> *I had a sandwich for **lunch**.*
> But:
> ***The breakfast** they gave us was awful.*
> *They all had **a delicious lunch**.*
> ***The meal** was perfect.*

H *Last* and *next*

> *These flats were built **last year**.*
> *The party is **next Saturday**.*
> But: ***the** previous **year**, **the** year before**, **the** following **Saturday**, (**the**) next **day**.*

TIP

When seen from the present: *yesterday, tomorrow* (no article). When seen from the past: ***the** day before/after* (with article).

101 Names

A Names of people and most place
names are without *the*.

> *Lucy   Mr Smith   Doctor Fry*
> *Texas   South Wales   Oxford University*

In some contexts we use an article.

> ***The** Lucy I know has got dark hair.*
> (the person called Lucy)
> *There's **a** Plymouth in the US.*
> (a place called Plymouth)

B Some place names have *the*, but others
do not.

> ***the** Black Sea   Lake Superior*

Whether a name has *the* or not
depends on the place (e.g. a sea or a
lake) and the structure of the name.

We often use *the* in these patterns.
Of-phrase: ***the** Isle **of** Wight*
Adjective: ***the American** School*
Plural: ***the** West **Indies***
We do not use *the* before a name in the
possessive form.

> ***Cleopatra's** Needle*

C Look at these examples.

- **Continents**: *a trip to Africa*
- **Countries**: *in Spain* (but *the* with plurals
  or names with *republic* or *kingdom*: ***the**
  Netherlands, **the** Czech Republic*)
- **States/Counties**: *through Ohio*

- **Regions** (two words): *in Central Asia*
  (but *the* with one word: *the South*)
- Most **mountains**: *on (Mount) Everest*
  (but *the* with ranges: *the Alps*)
- **Lakes**: *by Lake Erie* (but *the* with **rivers**,
  canals and **seas**: *the (River) Avon*)
- **Towns/cities**: *Sydney* (but *The Hague*)
- **Roads** and **streets**: *along Broadway*
  (but e.g. *The Avenue*, and *the Bath
  Road* meaning 'the road to Bath')
- **Parks**: *near Hyde Park*
- Some **bridges**: *on Tower Bridge* (but
  others have *the*: *the Humber Bridge*,
  and *the* with US bridges)
- **Stations**, **schools**, and other important
  buildings: *to Heathrow Airport, at
  Essex University, Leeds Town Hall* (but
  the with an of-phrase or adjective: *the
  University of Essex, the White House*)
- **Theatres**, **hotels**, **museums**, etc:
  *the Apollo Theatre, the Ritz Hotel,
  the Science Museum,* (but not with
  a possessive or a place name: *at
  Claridge's Hotel, in York Museum*)
- **Shops**: *shopping in Harrod's* (but *the*
  with a modifier: *The Kitchen Shop*)
- **Pubs**: *The Red Lion*

TIP
Study the patterns with *the* in B. Don't
put *the* before a name unless it has one
of these patterns or you know that *the*
is correct.

Possessives

A These are the forms of the possessive
determiners and pronouns.

Person	Determiners	Pronouns
Singular		
First	*my* book	*mine*
Second	*your* number	*yours*
Third	*his* father	*his*
	her decision	*hers*
	its location	
Plural		
First	*our* house	*ours*
Second	*your* coats	*yours*
Third	*their* attitude	*theirs*

His is male, and *her* is female.
   Ben's/**his** pen   Emma's/**her** dad
Its refers to something not human.
   the roof of the car / **its** roof
   the country's exports / **its** exports

B We use possessives for a connection,
often the fact that someone has
something.
   my bag (the bag that belongs to me)

Possessive determiners come before a
noun.
   Have you got ***your diary***?
We use a pronoun on its own without
a noun.
   I've got my diary. Have you got ***yours***?
   Those CDs are ***mine***.

C We normally use a possessive with people's heads, arms, etc, and their clothes.

> *He had **his** hands in **his** pockets.*
> *I've hurt **my** back.*
> (NOT *I've hurt ~~the back~~.*)

But when a person (e.g. *me*) is the object of the sentence, we use *the*.

> *Someone pushed **me** in **the** back.*

D *My friend* is a definite person, **the** person I am friends with. For **a** person I am friends with, we say *one of my friends* or *a friend of mine*. Here are some more examples with *of* + pronoun.

> *I like this band. I'm **a fan of theirs**.*
> *My private life is **no business of yours**.*

We can also use a possessive form after *of*.

> *We met **a cousin of Nicola's**.*

E We can use *own* after a possessive determiner.

> *I'd love to have **my own flat**.*
> (a flat that is mine and no one else's)
> *You'll have to make **your own bed**.*
> (make your bed yourself)

There is also a pattern with *of*.

> *I'd love a flat **of my own**.*

TIP

Don't use an apostrophe with determiners and pronouns. Don't write ~~your's~~. And remember that *it's* means *it is* or *it has*.

Demonstratives

A We use demonstratives to 'point to' something in the situation.

> ***This colour*** *is nice.*
> ***That house*** *there is for sale.*
> ***These flowers*** *are lovely.*
> *There's snow up there on* ***those hills***.

This and these refer to things near the speaker and *that* and *those* to things further away. *This* and *that* are singular. *These* and *those* are plural. We also use *this* and *that* with uncountable nouns.

> *this coffee   that music*

B We sometimes leave out the noun.

> *Look at these bags.* ***This*** *is nice.*
> *I like these jeans. ~ I like* ***those*** *better.*

We can also use *one/ones*.

> ***This one*** *is nice.   I like* ***those ones***.

C The meanings of 'near' and 'further away' apply to time as well as place.

> *I'm busy just at* ***this moment***. (now)
> *It's different* ***these days***. (now)
> *At* ***that time*** *I had no money.* (then)
> *Life was hard in* ***those days***. (then)

When we are in a place or situation, we use *this* to refer to it.

> ***This town*** *has absolutely no night life.*
> *How long is* ***this weather*** *going to last?*

We use *this* for something about to happen and *that* when it is over.

> *I'm going to enjoy **this meal**.*
> ***That** was delicious.*

D When we mention something again, we use *it/them* rather than a demonstrative.

> *This is a great party, isn't **it**?*
> *These socks are wet. I can't wear **them**.*

E We can use a demonstrative with people.

> *It was **that waiter** who took our order.*
> ***This** is my friend Amy. ~ Hello, Amy.*

F *That* can refer to a statement made before.

> *I'm not a member. ~ **That** doesn't matter.*
> *The rooms are big. **That**'s why it's cold.*
> *We're not made of money. ~ **That**'s true.*

G We can use *that* or *those* in a rather formal pattern.

> *I knew the voice as **that** of my sister.*
> *Some leaves are poisonous, especially **those** of evergreen shrubs.*
> (the leaves of evergreen shrubs)

TIP

On the phone use *this* to identify yourself. Say *Hello. This is Anna.* To ask who the other person is, say *Who is this?*

207

Introduction to quantifiers

A What is a quantifier?

A quantifier is a word like *many, no,* or *some*.

many times   **no** tickets   **some** water

A quantifier says how many/much. For example, *many* means a large quantity. The choice of quantifier can depend on whether a noun is countable or not. ➤ 105

A quantifier can be more than one word.

lots of fun   **a few** people

Some can have an adverb of degree.

too many emails   **quite a lot of** money
almost all the tickets   **very little** time

We can use a quantifier without a noun.

Most shops are open late, but **some** *close at five.* **A few** *close at six.*

Of must have a noun phrase or *it/them* after it.

A lot (**of the stores/of them**) *open late.*

We use *none* (not *no*) without a noun.

None *were open.*

B Large and small quantities

Here are some examples.

A large quantity:

a lot of / lots of letters
many questions   **much** discussion
a large number of accidents
numerous delays   **a great deal of** work

A neutral quantity:
some money *a number of* companies
A small quantity:
a few books *a little* oil *several* people
a small number of cases
a small amount of electricity
Zero quantity:
no work there is*n't any* bread

C Whole and part quantities

To talk about these quantities, we can
use words like *all* and *most*. ➤ 106
*The story is in **all** (**of**) the papers.*
*The bed takes up **most of** the space.*
***Half** (**of**) the audience were asleep.*
We often use *of*.

We can use large/small quantifiers
with *of* + determiner to express a
whole/part meaning. Compare these
examples.
*I found **some** information.*
(an amount)
***Some of the** information was irrelevant.*
(a part of the total)

We use *none* (not *no*) with *of*.
***None of** my friends went to the party.*

TIP
We can use the whole/part pattern with
a singular noun, e.g. *I've read **some of
this book**.*

105

A lot of, many, much, etc

A *A lot of, lots of, many,* and *much*
express a large quantity. We use *a
lot of* and *lots of* with a plural or
uncountable noun.

> We get ***a lot of visitors / lots of visitors.***
> You'll have ***a lot of fun / lots of fun.***

Many goes with a plural noun and
much with an uncountable noun.

> There aren't **many trains** on Sunday.
> There isn't **much traffic** on Sunday.

B As a general rule, we use *a lot of* and
lots of in positive statements and *many*
or *much* in negatives and questions.

> We **get a lot of** visitors.
> We **don't get many** visitors.
> **Do** you get **many** visitors?

But there are exceptions. In positive
statements we use *many* or *much* after
very, so, too, as, and *how.*

> **Very many** crimes go unreported.
> You're making **too much** noise.

A lot of and *lots of* are used more in
informal English (even in negatives
and questions), and *many* and *much*
are used in positive statements in more
formal English.

> We don't get ***a lot of*** visitors.
> ***Much*** criticism has been expressed.

C *A few, a little,* and *a bit of* express a
small quantity and are used mainly in
positive statements.
  *I took **a few photos**.*
  *I've got a **little money** / a **bit of money**.*
  A few goes with a plural noun and *a
  little* / *a bit of* with an uncountable noun.
  A bit of is more informal than *a little*.

D *Few* and *little* without *a* have a negative
meaning. Compare these examples.
  Is this a holiday area? ~
  ***Yes,** there are **a few** tourists.*
  (some tourists / a small number of
  tourists)
  ***No,** there are **few** tourists.*
  (not many tourists)
  *Even at 3 a.m. there was **a little** traffic.*
  (some traffic)
  *It was 3 a.m. so there was **little** traffic.*
  (not much traffic)

E *Many, few,* and *little* sometimes come
after a determiner, e.g. *his, the*.
  *Tim was with one of **his many** girlfriends.*
  ***The few** hotels in the area are full.*

  We can use *very* before *few* or *little*.
  *There are **very few** tourists here.*

  TIP
  We often use *a few* in phrases of time,
  e.g. *I'm here for **a few days**. I'll be back
  in **a few minutes**.*

106

All, most, etc

A We can use *all* or *most* to make a generalization.

> ***All rabbits*** *love green food.*
> ***Most pollution*** *could be avoided.*

Compare these examples.

> ***Most people*** *want a quiet life.*
> (people in general)
> *I know **most of the people** here.*
> (a specific group of people)

We can express 'most' in other ways.

> ***A/The majority of clubs*** *have a website.*
> *I know **more than half (of) the guests**.*

B Referring to a specific group, we use
all/most/half/none + *of* + determiner
+ noun.

> ***All (of) our rabbits*** *died.*
> ***Most of the pubs*** *in town serve food.*
> (NOT *the most of the pubs*)
> ***Half (of) the audience*** *were asleep.*
> ***None of these jackets*** *fit me any more.*

We cannot leave out *of* after *most* or
none. We can leave it out after *all* and
half, but not before a pronoun.

> *The rabbits got sick.* ***All of them*** *died.*
> *I started the book. I read **half of it**.*

We can use *a/an* with *half*.

> *We waited **half an hour**.*

We can use *all* after an object pronoun.
> *The rabbits died. We lost **them all** / all of them.*

It can also come in mid position.
> *The rabbits **all** died. / They **all** died.*

We can use *mostly* (but not *most*) in mid position.
> *The pubs in town **mostly** serve food.*

C *None* means 'not any of the group'.
> ***None of the rabbits** survived, I'm afraid.*
> (NOT ~~All of the rabbits didn't survive.~~)

Not all means 'fewer/less than all'.
> ***Not all (of) the rabbits** died. Some of them survived.*

D We can use *whole* as an adjective before a singular noun.
> *Did you watch **the whole game**?*
> (NOT ~~the all game~~)
> ***This whole idea** is crazy.*
> *You didn't eat **a whole chicken**!*

We can also use *whole* as a noun.
> *Did you watch **the whole of the game**?*

TIP

Do not confuse *all day* and *every day*. *We spent **all day** on the beach* means that we were there from morning till evening. *We spent **every day** on the beach* means that we went there each day of our holiday.

---

107 Both, either, neither, every, and each

A *Both, either,* and *neither* mean two things.
*Police closed the street at **both ends**.*
(one end **and** the other)
*I'm lucky. I can write with **either hand**.*
(one hand **or** the other)
***Neither of the twins** can walk yet.*
(**not** one twin **and not** the other)

B We use *both* with a plural noun.
***Both houses** are for sale.*
***Both (of) the houses** are for sale.*
***Both her parents** are out of work.*
But we do not say *the both houses.*

We can use an object pronoun + *both.*
*Two prisoners escaped, but the police
caught **them both** / **both of them**.*
Both can also come in mid position.
*The teams are **both** confident.*

C We use *either* or *neither* + singular
noun.
***Either way is** as good as the other.*
***Neither car is** economical to run.*

In positions other than the subject we
use *not ... either* rather than *neither.*
*I **don't** like **either** of those pictures.*
But *neither* can be the subject.
***Neither** of those pictures appeals to me.*

D We use *every* or *each* + singular noun
for all the members of a group.
*There were flags on **every/each house**.*
***Every/Each minute** the tension grew.*

Every/each + noun has a singular verb.
***Every/Each customer** is greeted.*

E In many contexts either *every* or *each* is
possible, but there is a difference. *Every
child* means all the children and implies
a large number. *Each child* means all
the children individually, one by one.
***Every child** needs love and attention.*
***Each child** had his/her photo taken.*
Each refers to two or more; *every* to
three or more.
*United scored in **each half** / both halves.*
*People came running from **every
direction** / all directions.*

F We can use *each* but not *every* in these
patterns.
***Each of the students** has a personal tutor.*
*We gave **them each** / **each of them** a kiss.*
*The winners **each** received a prize.*
*The tickets are £20 **each**.*
But we can use *each/every one (of)*.
***each one** / **every one** of the students*

TIP

Use *every* for things happening regularly,
e.g. *I go swimming **every Friday**. The
meetings are **every four weeks**.*

108

Some and *any*

A *Some/any* for a quantity

Some + plural or uncountable noun is
equivalent to *a/an* + singular noun.

> You'll need **some** wood, **a** hammer, and
> **some** nails.

Some is a positive quantity. We use *any*
mainly in negatives and questions.
Positive: *I've got **some** nails.*
Negative: *I haven't got **any** nails.*
Question: *Have you got **any/some**
nails?*

We use *any* with other negative words.

> *I **never** seem to have **any** money.*
> *We've won **hardly any** games this year.*

Any is the usual choice in questions.

> *Did you catch **any** fish? ~ Yes, lots. / No.*

But we use *some* for a more positive
tone, especially in offers and requests.

> *Did you catch **some** fish?*
> *Would you like **some** cornflakes?*

In an if-clause we can use either.

> *If you need **some/any** help, let me know.*

B *Someone*, etc

We choose between *someone/anyone*,
etc in the same way as *some/any*.

> ***Someone** has been trying to kill me.*
> *I haven't got **anything** to wear.*
> *Could you do **something** for me?*

C *Some/any* for a part quantity

Compare these two uses of *some*.
> There were **some people** in the studio.

Quantity: /səm/ 'a number of people'
> **Some people** enjoy quiz shows.

Part: /sʌm/ 'some but not all'

Here *some/any* means a part.
> **Some trains** have a restaurant car.
> **Some fish** can change their sex.
> **Some of the trains** were cancelled.
> **Some of the fish** in the tank were a beautiful blue colour.
> I like **some jazz** but not all of it.
> I didn't watch **any of the game**.

When *some* means a part, we can use it in a negative sentence.
> **Some people don't** enjoy quiz shows.

D *Any*

When *any* means 'it doesn't matter which', we can use it in positive sentences.
> You can choose **any colour** you like.
> Come **any time**. I'm always here.
> **Anyone** could just walk in here.

TIP

A phrase with *some* + singular noun can help you to be vague about details, e.g.
*The flight was delayed for **some reason**.*
*You must come and see me **some time**.*

109

Enough, some more, etc

A Enough

We can use *enough* with a plural or uncountable noun.

> There aren't **enough chairs**.
> Is there **enough room** for all of us?

We can use *of* for a part quantity.

> I've seen **enough of this film**.

B Plenty of and too many/much

Plenty of means 'enough' or 'more than enough'.

> There are **plenty of jobs** available.
> Don't rush. We've got **plenty of time**.

For 'more than enough' as a bad thing, we use *too many/much*.

> You always take **too many clothes** on holiday. Why take so many?
> I put **too much salt** in the soup.

C Another and some more

These express an extra quantity. We use *another* with a singular noun and *some more* with a plural or uncountable noun.

> Would you like **another sausage**?
> Have **some more carrots**.
> I'll get **some more orange juice**.

In some contexts (➤ 108A) we use *any*.

> There isn't **any more orange juice**.

Another can also mean 'a different one'.
  *I'm going to buy **another computer** to
  replace this one.*

Before *more* we can also use *a lot, lots,
many, much, a few, a little,* and *a bit.*
  *I've got **lots more** jobs to do after this.*
  *Can't you put **a bit more** effort into it?*

D Other

Other is an adjective meaning
'different' or 'not the one just
mentioned'.
  *We crossed to **the other side** of the road.*
  *Sarah was there, but I didn't know any
  of **the other guests**.*

We can use *other* without a noun to
refer to a thing or a person.
  *Take one bag. Give me **the other** (one).*
  *One twin is taller than **the other** (one).*
We can use *others* without a noun for
more than one.
  *Some pubs serve food, but **others** don't.*
  *I'm early. The **others** will be here soon.*

Number + *other* means an extra quantity.
  *There are **four other**/four more rooms
  upstairs.*

TIP

You can use *another* in a phrase
expressing an extra period of time, e.g.
*I'm staying on **for another three days** /
for three more days.*

110

Personal pronouns

A Subject and object forms

These are the forms.

Person	Singular		Plural	
	SUBJ.	OBJ.	SUBJ.	OBJ.
First	*I*	*me*	*we*	*us*
Second	*you*	*you*	*you*	*you*
Third	*he*	*him*	*they*	*them*
	she	*her*		
	it	*it*		

For meaning and use, ➤ 111.

We use the subject form for the subject of a finite clause.

*I know Gemma. **She**'s in my class.*

We use the object form for the object of a verb or preposition.

*These notes are for Matthew. Could you give **them** to **him**, please?*

We use the object form for a pronoun on its own. Compare these answers.

*Who said that? ~ **Me**. / I did.*

We also use the object form after *be*.

*It wasn't **me** who made the mistake.*

B *And*/*or* with pronouns

We can use *and* or *or* to combine a pronoun with a noun phrase or another pronoun.

***Elaine and I** are good friends.*
*Sam could have rung **you or me**.*

We normally put *I*/*me* after *and*.
(NOT ~~I and Elaine~~)

220

C Nouns and pronouns

We do not usually use a pronoun
together with a noun.

Gemma is in my class.
(NOT *Gemma she's in my class.*)

But in informal speech we can use this
pattern to emphasize a topic.

***Your brother, he** makes me laugh.*
***Those new students**, I just saw **them**.*

We make clear what the topic is before
we continue with the message.

We can also use the following pattern
in informal speech.

***She**'s in my class, **Gemma** (is).*
*I just saw **them**, **those new students**.*

D Noun or pronoun?

Compare these sentences.

*Matt was picked to play, but **he** was ill.*
*Matt and Tom were picked to play, but
Matt was ill.*

We use a pronoun (*he*) when the
reference is clear. We use a noun
(*Matt*) when a pronoun would not be
clear.

TIP

After *and*, choose the pronoun form as
if it was on its own. You say ***I'm** going
out*, so say ***Leo and I** are going out*. You
say *Come with **me***, so say *Come with
Amber and me*.

---

111 The use of pronouns

A *He*, *she*, and *it*

He/him, *she/her*, and *it* are singular.
He means a male person, *she* a female
person, and *it* means something not
human.

> Invite Mark. **He**'s great fun. I like **him**.
> Invite Anna. **She**'s great fun. I like **her**.
> That tune is good. **It**'s catchy. I like **it**.

We use *it* not only for things but
also for animals, actions, situations,
feelings, and ideas.

> What's that? Is **it** a beetle?
> We got lost. **It** was awful.
> They were cheating. I knew **it**.

For *it* as an empty subject, ➤ 24.

We also use *it* for an unknown person
when we talk about identity.

> There's the phone. **It** might be Debbie.
> Who broke this glass? ~ **It** was Paul.

B *They*

They/them refers to people and things.

> I like your cousins. **They**'re great fun.
> I like these pictures. **They**'re nice.

We can use *they* for other people in
general, or for the authorities.

> **They** say we need to save energy.
> **They**'re going to increase taxes.

C A person of unknown sex

We can refer to such a person like this.

*When the winner is known, **he or she**
should make **his or her** way to the stage.*

It is regarded as sexist to only use *he*
and *his* here. *They* can be used for a
single person of unknown sex.

*When the winner is known, **they** should
make **their** way to the stage.*

D *We*

We/us means *me* and one or more
others. It can include *you*.

__We__'re late. ~ Yes, we are.
(we = you and I)
__We__'re late. ~ Yes, you are.
(we = he/she/they and I)

We can also mean people in general.

*__We__ know that the ice caps are melting.
Language enables **us** to communicate.*

E *You*

We use *you* for the person or people
spoken to, or for people in general.

*__You__ can wear anything to the theatre.
How do **you** train a police dog?*

TIP

One meaning people in general,
including the speaker, is rather formal.
Say *I hope so*, rather than *One hopes so*.

112 Reflexive and emphatic pronouns

A We form the pronouns with *self/selves*.

Person	Singular	Plural
First	*myself*	*ourselves*
Second	*yourself*	*yourselves*
Third	*himself*	
	herself	} *themselves*
	itself	

B We use a reflexive pronoun as an object referring back to the subject.
   *I blamed **myself** for the accident.*
   *Luke is teaching **himself** Italian.*
   *The country declared **itself** independent.*

C Look at these examples.
   *I didn't have my passport with **me**.*
   *My mother likes the family all around **her**.*

We use the personal pronoun when it clearly refers to the subject (*I*, *my mother*). But we sometimes need a reflexive to make the meaning clear.
   *Sue read an article about **herself**.*
   (about Sue, not someone else)

We also use a reflexive after combinations with a preposition.
   *One man was **talking to himself**.*
   *I was **annoyed with myself**.*

D There are some idiomatic uses.
   Enjoy yourselves. (have a good time)
   *Please **help yourself.*** (take e.g. food)
   *I was **by myself**/on my own.* (alone)

E Some verbs taking a reflexive in other
   languages do not do so in English.
   *I **feel** ill. Can't you **remember**?*
   *I **got up** early. Please **sit down**.*
   Other verbs like this include: *complain,
   concentrate, hurry, lie down, relax, rest,
   stand up, wonder, worry.*

F We use emphatic pronouns to
   emphasize a noun phrase.
   *The President **himself** welcomed us.*
   *I **myself** have no opinion on the matter.*
   The pronoun can mean 'without help'.
   *We built the house **ourselves**.*

G Note also *each other / one another.*
   *We should all help **one another**.*
   *Jane and Amy smiled at **each other**.*
   This means that Jane smiled at Amy,
   and Amy smiled at Jane.

   Compare the reflexive pronoun.
   *The acrobats fell and hurt **themselves**.*
   *The two boxers hurt **each other**.*

TIP

Say *I must wash / I must have a bath*
and *I must get changed*. A reflexive is
less usual with these verbs.

113 *One* and *ones*

A We sometimes use *one* or *ones* instead
of a noun.

*Which is your coat? ~ This **one**.*
*A blue pen or a black **one**?*
This television is a bit bigger than the
***one** we had before.*
*These two houses are the only **ones** in*
the street with gardens
*Get some tomatoes – small **ones**.*

We use *one/ones* to avoid repeating a
noun. *One* is singular and *ones* is plural.

We cannot do this with an uncountable
noun, but we can leave out the noun.
*Do you prefer pop music or **classical**?*

B In some patterns we can either replace
the noun with *one/ones* or simply
leave it out.

- After a demonstrative
  *Look at these rings. **This** (**one**) is nice.*
- After *each, any, other, either*, and *neither*
  ***Each** (**one**) of these patterns is different.*
  Don't lose that key because I haven't got
  ***another** (**one**).*
  *There are two choices, and **neither***
  *(**one**) appeals to me.*
- After *which*
  I couldn't answer all the questions. ~
  ***Which** (**ones**) did you find difficult?*
- After a superlative
  *These photos are the **nicest** (**ones**).*

C In some patterns we cannot leave out
one/ones.

- After an adjective
  *I had an accident but not a **serious one**.*
- After *the*
  *These sweets are **the ones** I like.*
- After *every*
  *We've been on several trips, and **every
  one** was enjoyable.*

D We can replace *a/an* + noun with *one*.
*I've got a map if you need **one**.* (a map)
*I'm not used to weddings. I haven't been
to **one** for ages.* (a wedding)

Compare *one/some* and *it/they*.
*I haven't got a backpack. I'll have to buy
one.* (a backpack)
*I haven't got any boots. I'll have to buy
some.* (some boots)
*I've got a backpack. You can borrow **it** if
you like.* (the backpack)
*I've got some boots, but **they** might not
fit you.* (the boots)

TIP

We can sometimes leave out *one/ones*
when we use two adjectives, e.g. *Is this
the old price or the **new** (one)? We've
got French books and **German** (ones).*
We can also leave out *one/ones* after an
adjective of colour, e.g. *My toothbrush
is the **blue**.*

114

Everyone, something, etc

A *Every, some, any, no* form compounds
with *-one/-body* and *-thing*, and
adverbs with *-where.*
*I saw **someone/somebody** outside.*
*Is there **anything** on television?*
*I've looked **everywhere** for that receipt.*

B *Everyone/everybody* means 'all the people'.
***Everyone** watched in amazement.*
Someone/somebody means 'a person'.
***Someone**'s left all this litter here.*
No one/nobody means 'no people'.
***Nobody** wants to take such a risk.*

C We use *-thing* for things, actions, etc.
*I've got **everything** I need, thank you.*
***Something** was happening at last.*
*Just keep quiet and say **nothing**.*

D *Everywhere* means '(in) all places'.
*There are advertisements **everywhere**.*
Somewhere means '(in) a place'.
*Have you put my bag **somewhere**?*
Nowhere means '(in) no places'.
*There's **nowhere** to sit down.*

E We choose between *someone/anyone*,
etc as between *some/any.* ➤ 108A, 108D.
*There's **someone** at the door.*
*I'm not expecting **anyone**.*
*We can go **anywhere** you like.*

F *-one/-body* has a possessive form.
> *The guide had **everyone's** passports.*
> *I can get a lift in **somebody's** car.*

G We can use an adjective or *else* after any of the compounds.
> *I heard **something interesting** today.*
> *Let's go **somewhere nice**.*
> *Have you got **anything cheaper**?*
> *Can I do **anything else** for you?*

We can also use a phrase or clause.
> ***Nobody in our group** speaks Greek.*
> *I've told you **everything I know**.*

We can use an adverb before a compound.
> *This plant will grow **almost anywhere**.*
> *I've done **absolutely nothing** wrong!*

H The compounds take a singular verb.
> ***Someone has** left a message.*
> ***Is everything** all right?*

After *-one/-body* we normally use *they/their* even with a singular verb.
> ***Everyone** was asked what **they** thought.*
> ***Somebody** has left **their** mobile here.*

TIP

If you want to be vague, then the informal phrase *or something*, meaning 'or something similar', can be useful, e.g. *For lunch I'll have a sandwich **or something**. Let's go for a walk **or something**.*

115 Introduction to adjectives

A Look at this example.

*These **excellent** apartments are in a **quiet residential** area.*

An adjective modifies a noun. The adjectives here express physical qualities (*quiet*) or an opinion (*excellent*), or they classify something (*residential*, so not *industrial*).

B An adjective always has the same form. There are no endings for number or gender.

*an **old** man   an **old** woman   **old** people*

But some adjectives can have comparative/superlative endings. ➤ 131

*My wife is **older** than I am.*

Most adjectives have no special form. But there are some endings used to form adjectives from other words, e.g. *residential, beautiful, cloudy.*

C We can use two or more adjectives together.

*a **beautiful white sandy** beach*

For the order of adjectives, ➤ 117.

We can put an adverb of degree (e.g. *very*) in front of most adjectives.

*a **very large** apartment*
*a **really beautiful** beach*

D One main position for an adjective is
'attributive' – before a noun.
*Canterbury is a **lovely** city.*
*A **noisy** party kept us awake.*

The other is 'predicative' – after a
linking verb such as *be*.
*Canterbury is **lovely**.*
*The party seemed very **noisy**.*

We can also sometimes put an
adjective after a noun. ➤ 116C

E Some adjectives can follow *as* or *than*.
*Let me know as soon **as possible**.*
*I went to bed later **than usual**.*

F We can sometimes use an adjective
immediately after a conjunction.
*Pick the fruit **when ripe**.*
(when it is ripe)
***If possible**, please send a photo.*
(if it is possible)

G In literary English you may see
examples like this.
***Uncertain**, the woman hesitated.*
*The weather, **bright and sunny**, had
brought everyone out of doors.*

TIP

Use an adjective to express approval or
enthusiasm: *We've got permission. ~
Oh, **good/great**. / That's **marvellous**.*

More about adjectives

A Attributive only

Some adjectives can go only in attributive position (before a noun).

*The project was an **utter** failure.*
*The **outer** door is locked at night.*
*The house is on a **main** road.*
(BUT NOT ~~The road is main.~~)

Attributive-only adjectives include:
chief, elder/est, eventual, former, inner, lone, main, mere, only, outer, own, principal, sheer, sole, upper, utter.

B Predicative only

Some adjectives can go only in predicative position (after a linking verb such as *be*).

*I was **pleased** to see my friends.*
*The children were soon **asleep**.*
(BUT NOT ~~the asleep children~~)

These words include:

- some with *a-*, e.g. *afraid, alike, alive, alone, asleep, awake*;
- some expressing feelings, e.g. *content, glad, pleased, upset.*

There is sometimes another word we can use before a noun.

*being **asleep*** / *a **sleeping** child*
*being **alive*** / *a **living** person*
*feeling **lonely/alone*** / *a **lonely** feeling*

Ashamed, glad, pleased, and *upset*
can come before a noun when not
referring directly to a person.
   the **glad** news   an **upset** stomach

C After a noun

Some adjectives can have a
prepositional phrase after them.
   *People were **anxious for news**.*
   *The box was **full of old clothes**.*

The adjective + prepositional phrase
can go directly after the noun.
   ***People anxious for news** kept ringing.*
   *I found **a box full of old clothes**.*
But we cannot put it before the noun.
   (NOT ~~a full of old clothes box~~)

Sometimes the position of the
adjective depends on the meaning.
   *The sum **involved** is small.* (relevant)
   *It's a rather **involved** story.* (complicated)
   *There were 65 people **present**.* (there)
   *Let's discuss the **present** situation.* (now)

Note also compound + adjective. ➤ 114G
   *You mustn't do **anything silly**.*

TIP

Well (in good health) and *ill* are not
often used before a noun. *How are you?
~ (I'm) very **well**, thank you. How's your
father? ~ I'm afraid he's **ill** / he's not
very **well** at the moment.*

117 The order of adjectives

A When two or more adjectives come
before a noun, there is often a fixed order.
*a **nice big warm** fire*
(NOT *a warm big nice fire*)
The order of adjectives depends
mainly on the kind of meaning they
express. An expression of opinion like
nice comes first.

B When we use an adjective and a noun
modifier, the adjective comes first.
*the **old town** wall   **dark winter** evenings*

C The modifiers usually go in the
following order, starting with group 1.
1   Opinion: *nice, excellent, awful,* etc
2   Size: *long, large, small, short,* etc
3   Most other qualities: *clear, busy,
    famous, friendly, soft, quiet,* etc
4   Age: *new, old*
5   Shape: *round, square, fat, narrow,* etc
6   Colour: *blue, red, white, black,* etc
7   Participle forms: *running, missing,
    covered, broken,* etc
8   Origin: *British, Italian, American,*
    etc
9   Material: *sandy, paper, plastic,* etc
10 Type: *electronic, human, chemical,
    money (problems),* etc
11 Purpose: *alarm (clock), tennis
    (court), walking (boots),* etc

Here are some examples.

*an **old cardboard** box* (age + material)
*a **new improved** model* (age + participle)
*a **small square** room* (size + shape)
*two **excellent public tennis** courts*
(opinion + type + purpose)

In general the word closest to the noun has the closest link with it. In the phrase *excellent public tennis courts*, the word *tennis* is closely connected with *courts*.

The rules are not absolute. We may prefer a short word before a long one.

*a **big horrible** building*

D A modifier can be a compound.

*an old **pale blue** football shirt*
*a powerful **high-speed** electric drill*

E With two similar adjectives, the shorter one usually comes first.

*a **bright, cheerful** smile*

Here we can also use *and*.

*a bright **and** cheerful smile*

And is not used with different meanings.

*a **lovely old** city*
(NOT ~~a lovely and old city~~)

TIP

We use *and* when the adjectives come after a verb like *be*, e.g. *The city is old **and** lovely.* An expression of opinion (*lovely*) comes last.

235

118

Tired and *exhausted*; *amusing* and *amused*, etc

A Ungradable adjectives

Most adjectives are gradable – they express qualities which can exist in different grades or degrees.

It's **very/extremely** warm today.
I feel **rather** tired/**a bit** tired now.

Some adjectives are ungradable. They express extreme qualities such as perfection. We cannot use words like *very* or *fairly* with an ungradable adjective, but we can use *absolutely*.

It's **absolutely boiling** today.
I feel **absolutely exhausted** now.

With some ungradable adjectives we can also use *completely* or *totally*.

I'm afraid that's **completely impossible**.
It's a **totally incredible** story.

Really and *so* go with both types.

I felt **really/so tired**.
I felt **really/so exhausted**.

For *quite* and *rather*, ➤ 128.

Other ungradable adjectives include: *absurd, amazed/ing, awful, brilliant, certain, delicious, delighted, dreadful, enormous, essential, excellent, false, fascinated/ing, horrible, huge, ideal, magnificent, marvellous, perfect, ridiculous, terrible, terrific, terrified/ing, thrilled/ing, useless, vast.*

B Adjectives in *-ing* and *-ed*

Look at these examples.

> *The film made me laugh a lot. It was really **amusing**.*
> *I talked to an **interesting** man.*
> *This weather is so **depressing**.*

Adjectives in *-ing* express the idea that something affects us. A film is *amusing* because it makes us laugh.

Compare the adjectives in *-ed*.

> *The audience laughed a lot. They were really **amused**.*
> *I was **interested** in the conversation.*
> *I feel **depressed** when it rains.*

Adjectives in *-ed* express the feelings we have about something. We are *amused* when we see something funny.

Other pairs of adjectives in *-ing* and *-ed* include: alarming/ed, amazing/ed, annoying/ed, boring/ed, confusing/ed, disappointing/ed, exciting/ed, fascinating/ed, frightening/ed, pleasing/ed, puzzling/ed, relaxing/ed, shocking/ed, surprising/ed, thrilling/ed, tiring/ed, worrying/ed.

TIP

Do not use *very* with an ungradable adjective like *excellent*. Say *it's excellent* or *it's very good* but not ~~*it's very excellent*~~.

237

The + adjective

A *The poor*, etc

We can use *the* + adjective to refer to some groups of people in society.

The poor lived in terrible conditions.
(poor people in general)

The young should respect *the old*.
(young/old people in general)

We can also say *poor people*, etc with the same general meaning.

Poor people lived in terrible conditions.

For a specific person or group of people, we use *man, people*, etc.

A young man welcomed us.
(NOT *A young welcomed us.*)

The old people have just left.
(NOT *The old have just left.*)

The + adjective takes a plural verb. But we do not add *-s* to the adjective.

The old are respected. (NOT *the olds*)

Other adjectives and participle forms used in this way are: *blind, dead, deaf, disabled, elderly, homeless, hungry, living, middle-aged, (under)privileged, rich, sick, sighted, strong, unemployed, weak*; and some nationality words, e.g. *the French*.

The adjective can have an adverb in front of it.

the *very* rich   the *severely* disabled

Some adjectives normally have an adverb in front of them.

> the **less** fortunate   the **mentally** ill

B *The supernatural*, etc

Some adjectives and participle forms can be used after *the* for things in general which have a particular abstract quality.

> Do you believe in **the supernatural**?
> It was a journey into **the unknown**.

We use a singular verb.

> **The new** drives out **the old**.

Some other words used in this way are *absurd, mysterious, unexplained*.

C *The unexpected*, etc

A few words can be used after *the* with a more specific meaning.

> I hate getting up in **the dark**.
> I fear **the worst** but hope for **the best**.
> You're asking **the impossible**.
> Have you heard **the latest** (news)?
> **The unexpected** sometimes happens.

TIP

Use *the* + adjective/participle + *thing* for a particular aspect of a situation, e.g. **The good thing** about friends is that you can trust them. **The annoying thing** was that I didn't have the money for a taxi.

120 Introduction to adverbials

A Adverbials add more details to a sentence. They tell us how, when, or where something happened.

Slowly the bus drove past.
We have now been waiting an hour.
I'm travelling around the world.

Often an adverbial is an extra element that could be left out of a sentence.

At last we were off. OR *We were off.*
But sometimes it is necessary to complete the sentence. ➤ 2D

Rick's been to the match.
The next performance is tomorrow.

B An adverbial can be a simple adverb (e.g. *there*, *carefully*).

No one lives there.
I wrapped all the glasses carefully.
We can put an adverb of degree (e.g. *very*) in front of the adverb.

The time passed very quickly.

An adverbial can also be a prepositional phrase (e.g. *to the park*).

We walked to the park.
The queue went round the block.
In a strange way, I don't mind failing.
We can use a noun phrase (e.g. *last week*), but this is less frequent.

I saw a great film last week.

C An adverbial can usually go in more than one place in a sentence.

> ***Naturally*** *we were expecting a call.*
> *We were **naturally** expecting a call.*
> *We were expecting a call, **naturally**.*

These places are front position, mid position, and end position. ➤ 121, 122

The best position for an adverbial may depend on what type it is (e.g. manner or time), or on its length. A long phrase goes better at the beginning or end.

> *I can't express it **in simple words**.*
> (NOT ~~I can't in simple words express it.~~)

Sometimes we put an adverbial in front position to link with the previous sentence.

> *I waited for ages. **In the end** I gave up and went home.*

D An adverbial can also follow a noun that it modifies.

> *The car **in front** braked suddenly.*
> *The rain **yesterday** spoilt our picnic.*

TIP

When there are two clauses, the position of the adverbial can affect the meaning. Compare:

*We agreed **immediately** that I would leave.* (an immediate agreement)
*We agreed that I would leave **immediately**.* (an immediate departure).

121 Adverbials: front and end position

A Front position

Front position is at the beginning.

Sure enough, there was a queue.

Just stop doing that, will you?

Most types of adverbial can go here.

If there is a conjunction, it goes before the adverbial.

I thought there would be a queue, **and** sure enough there was.

We often put an adverbial in front position to relate to something in the previous sentence.

I'm busy today. **Tomorrow** I'm free.

B End position

Sometimes an adverbial comes at the end of a clause.

It doesn't often rain **in the desert**.

Everyone thanked her **very warmly**.

Almost all types of adverbial can go here.

An adverbial usually follows an object.

I planned the trip **carefully**.

(NOT ~~I planned carefully the trip.~~)

But a short adverbial can go before a long object.

I planned **carefully** our trip around the States.

C Order in end position

Sometimes there is more than one adverbial in end position. Usually a shorter adverbial goes before a longer one.

*We sat **around most of the weekend**.*

An adverbial goes directly after a verb to which it is closely linked in meaning.

*I don't want to go **to work** today.*
*Why did you come **home** late?*

We usually put an adverbial of place next to *go, come*, etc.

Time and place adverbials go either way.

*I saw Simon **yesterday on the bus**.*
*I saw Simon **on the bus yesterday**.*

Adverbials of manner, time, and place usually come before frequency.

*I get to work **quite early, usually**.*
*I can do the puzzle **easily sometimes**.*

Mainly in writing, some types of adverb can come in end position, as an afterthought.

*He's been held up in traffic, **perhaps**.*
*My wallet was still there, **thankfully**.*

TIP

Do not put an adverb before a short object. Say *We did the job quickly*, not ~~We did quickly the job~~.

Adverbials: mid position

A An adverbial can be in mid position (close to the verb). The adverbial goes before a simple-tense verb.

> We **usually sit** over there.

The adverbial usually follows an auxiliary verb or the ordinary verb *be*.

> I've **always** liked curry.
> This song **is definitely** the best.

If a verb has two auxiliaries, mid position is usually after the first one.

> I've **just been** talking to Pete.

But adverbs of manner and some adverbs of degree come after the second auxiliary.

> The visitors are **being warmly** welcomed.
> We've **been completely** let down.

B Adverbials in mid position are usually one-word adverbs, or short phrases with adverbs of degree.

> I **always** call – I **hardly ever** forget.

Most longer phrases do not go in mid position.

> You play that song **all the time**.
> (NOT ~~You all the time play that song.~~)

But truth, comment, and linking adverbials can go in mid position.

> The day was **on the whole** a success.

This can be rather formal.

C Mid position adverbials usually follow
   an auxiliary or *be*. But they can go
   before a stressed auxiliary or emphatic
   do.

> You **obviously** ARE in love with her.
> I **never did** like flying.

Some adverbs (e.g. truth adverbs)
usually go before a negative auxiliary.

> I **certainly** haven't forgotten.
> It **probably** doesn't matter.

Others can come before or after the
negative auxiliary, with a change in
meaning.

> I **really don't** remember. (not at all)
> I **don't really** remember. (I'm unsure.)

If words are left out after the auxiliary,
the adverb goes before it.

> My wife gets up early, but I **never do**.
> Will you be in? ~ I **probably will**.

An adverb goes before *have to* and
ought to.

> You **never have to** wait long for a bus.
> We **definitely ought to** ask for our
> money back.

TIP

The position of adverbials is a complex
topic where there is no set of simple
rules. But reading and repeating the
example sentences will help you to get
a feel for this area of English.

123 Adverb forms

A We form many adverbs from an adjective + *-ly*, e.g. *fluent* (adj.) → *fluently* (adv.).

> Tony speaks French **fluently**.

For the spelling of adverbs in *-ly*, ➤ 177C, 178A.

Some adverbs have a form which is unrelated to other words. These include: *always, just, often, never, perhaps, quite, rather, seldom, soon, very*.

B Some adjectives end in *-ly*, e.g. *friendly, lovely*.

> We received a **friendly** greeting.

We cannot add another *-ly* to form an adverb. Instead we use a phrase with *manner, way*, or *fashion*.

> They waved in a **friendly** manner.

Or we use a different adverb with a similar meaning.

> She's a **lovely** dancer. (adjective)
> She dances **beautifully**. (adverb)

We can add *-ly* to an ing-form.

> It's **surprisingly** cold for August.

But we do not usually add *-ly* to a form in *-ed*, except *excitedly* and *exhaustedly*.

C Some adverbs have the same form as adjectives, e.g. *early, fast, hard, high, long, low, still, straight*.

Here are some examples.
*We caught the **fast** train.* (adjective)
*The train was going quite **fast**.* (adverb)

*We didn't have a **long** wait.* (adjective)
*We didn't have to wait **long**.* (adverb)

D Some adverbs can be with or without
-ly, e.g. *cheap(ly)*, *direct(ly)*, *fair(ly)*,
slow(ly), *tight(ly)*.
*I came as **quick/quickly** as I could.*
The form without *-ly* is more informal
and used only in frequent combinations.
*You'd better **go slow**/slowly along here.*
BUT *He opened the parcel **slowly**.*

E Some pairs (e.g. *hard, hardly*) are both
adverbs but have different meanings.
*You're working too **hard**.*
*There's **hardly** any time.* (almost no time)
*I went to bed **late**.*
*I haven't seen Donna **lately**.* (recently)
Other pairs include: *deep, deeply*; *free,
freely*; *high, highly*; *near, nearly*.

F *Good* is an adjective, and *well* is the
equivalent adverb.
*He's a **good** player. / He plays **well**.*
For *well* as an adjective, ➤ 116 Tip.

TIP

Hourly, daily, weekly, and *monthly*
(from *hour, day,* etc) can be adjectives
or adverbs: *A **daily** newspaper is
published **daily**.*

247

124 Adverbials of manner

A Adjectives and adverbs

Look at these examples.

*We found an **easy** solution.*
*You must be **sensible**.*

An adjective (*easy*, *sensible*) comes before a noun or after a linking verb such as *be*. ➤ 115D

Now look at the adverbs.

*We solved the problem **easily**.*
*Try to act **sensibly**.*

An adverb of manner says how something happens. It usually comes after a verb (*act*) or a verb + object (*solved the problem*). Most are formed from an adjective + *-ly*. ➤ 123

B Linking verb and action verb

Compare the verbs in these sentences.
Linking verb + adjective:

*The official **was polite**.*

Action verb + adverb:

*The official **listened politely**.*
(NOT *He listened polite.*)

A linking verb is one like *be*, *become*, *feel*, *look*, *seem*. An action verb is one like *argue*, *drive*, *meet*, *listen*, *work*.

Some verbs can be of either type.

*He **looked nervous**.* (appeared)
*He **looked nervously** at us.* (directed his eyes)

*The atmosphere **grew tense**.* (became)
*The tree **grew rapidly**.* (increased in size)

C Prepositional phrases of manner

We can use a prepositional phrase.
*I chose my words carefully / **with care**.*
*He stared at me rather aggressively / **in a rather aggressive manner**.*
*The winning numbers are chosen randomly / **at random**.*

D Position

An adverbial of manner usually goes in end position.
*The sun still shone **brightly**.*
*We continued our work **in silence**.*

A one-word adverb can sometimes come in mid position. ➤ 122
*I **quickly** ran and got my coat.*
It can sometimes come in front position for emphasis.
***Gently** fry the banana pieces.*
The last two examples are more common in writing than in speech.

TIP

If a verb has a similar meaning to *be*, then it's a linking verb and is followed by an adjective rather than an adverb. *She **seemed**/**looked** excited* is close in meaning to *She **was** excited*.

125 Adverbials of place/time

A Position

These adverbials often go in end position.

> *It's my birthday **tomorrow**.*
> *There was an accident **on the motorway**.*

For more than one adverbial, ➤ 121C.

Adverbials of place and time can also go in front position.

> ***On Saturday** we're going to London.*

Some short adverbials of time can go in mid position.

> *I've **just** remembered something.*

These include: *already, finally, immediately, no longer, now, soon, then.*

B Yet

Yet comes at the end of a question or negative.

> *Have you left **yet**? I haven't got up **yet**.*

In mid position it is a little formal.

> *We have not **yet** replied.*

C Still

In positive statements and questions, *still* goes in mid position.

> *I'm **still** waiting for a taxi.*
> *Is your grandfather **still** working?*

In negative statements it goes before the auxiliary.

> *The child **still** hasn't learned to read.*

250

D *Already*

Already goes mainly in mid position.

    *I've **already** had breakfast.*

    *Have you **already** done your project?*

Front or end position is more emphatic.

    *Is it lunch time **already**? How time flies.*

E *No longer*

No longer goes in mid position and is a little formal.

    *These products are **no longer** made.*

Compare *any longer / any more*.

    *They don't make them **any longer/more**.*

F *Long* and *far*

We use these adverbs in questions and negatives and with *too*, *so*, *as*, and *enough*.

    *Will you be **long**? It's not **far** to walk.*

    *The speech went on **too long**.*

Compare these positive statements.

    *I had to wait **a long time**.*

    *It's **a long way** to walk.*

G *After* and *afterwards*

We use *afterwards* or *after that* as an adverb rather than *after*.

    *We discussed the film **afterwards**.*

But we say *the day after*, *soon after*, etc.

    *I ordered a CD and it came **the day after**.*

TIP

An adverbial can also modify a noun, e.g. *Exports **last year** broke all records.*

126 Adverbials of frequency

A An adverb of frequency says how often something happens. It usually goes in mid position.

> We **sometimes** eat out.
> The bus doesn't **usually** stop here.
> I can **never** open these packets.

These adverbs include: *always*; *normally*, *usually*; *often*, *frequently*; *sometimes*, *occasionally*; *seldom*, *rarely*; *never*, *ever*.

B In mid position, *sometimes*, *occasionally*, and *frequently* go before a negative auxiliary.

> I **sometimes don't** have any lunch.

As a general rule, *always*, *often*, *normally*, and *usually* go after the negative auxiliary.

> You **can't always** get a seat on the bus.
> I **don't normally** come this way.

C Some adverbs of frequency can go in front or end position.

> **Normally** I tip my hairdresser.
> We all make mistakes **sometimes**.

These adverbs are *normally*, *usually*, *generally*, *frequently*, *sometimes*, and *occasionally*.

Often can go in end position, especially with *very* or *quite*. *A lot* takes end position.

> Do you come here **often/a lot**?
> I see Laura quite **often**/quite **a lot**.

In instructions, *always* and *never* go in front position.

> **Always** *switch the machine off after use.*
> **Never** *leave luggage unattended.*

D *Never* (= not ever) is a negative word.

> *We **never** ask for your password.*
> (We do**n't** ever ask for your password.)

We use *ever* mainly in questions.

> *Have you **ever** been to Australia?*

We also use it with negative words.

> *I would**n't** ever do a thing like that.*
> ***Nothing* ever** happens in this place.*

Or we can use it in a condition or a comparison.

> *If you **ever** want a chat, just drop in.*
> *The river was higher **than** I'd **ever** seen it.*

E We can use a phrase with *every*, *most*, or *some* in front or end position.

> ***Every summer*** *we all go sailing together.*
> *The postman calls **most days**.*
> ***Some mornings*** *it's hard to get up.*

We also use *once*, *twice*, *three times*, etc in this pattern.

> *The group meets **once a month**.*
> *One tablet to be taken **three times a day**.*

TIP

Seldom and *rarely* are a little formal.
Instead of *I **seldom** watch TV*, say *I
do**n't** often watch TV*.

---

127 Adverbs of degree

A We can use an adverb of degree before
an adjective or before another adverb.

*It's a **very** simple idea.*
*It's getting **a bit** hot in here.*
*The time passed **quite** quickly.*
*We must leave **fairly** soon.*

These adverbs include: *absolutely,
completely, totally; extremely, very,
really, awfully, too; fairly, pretty,
quite, rather, somewhat; a bit, a little,
slightly; hardly, (not) at all.*

B *Somewhat, a little, a bit,* and *slightly*
usually go with undesirable qualities.

*The journey was **somewhat stressful**.*
(NOT *The journey was somewhat
enjoyable.*)

But we can use a desirable quality with
the comparative form.

*I was feeling **somewhat better**.*

Other adverbs that can go before a
comparative include: *a bit, a little, a
lot, any, much, no, rather, slightly.*

*Let's try to go **a bit** faster.*
*This gadget makes the job **much** easier.*

C An adverb of degree can modify a verb.

*I was **nearly** dying of thirst.*
*Do you **really** think so?*
*The man **absolutely** refused to move.*

Those in mid position include:
*absolutely, almost, completely, hardly,
just, nearly, quite, rather, really, totally.*
Some can also go in end position.
 *I forgot the time **completely**.*

Almost, just, and *nearly* go before a
negative auxiliary.
 *I **just** don't understand, I'm afraid.*

These adverbs always go in end
position: *a bit, a little, a lot, awfully,
more, (the) most, terribly.*
 *First impressions matter **a lot**.*
 *I miss you **terribly**.*

We can use *(very) much* in a negative
sentence or question.
 *I didn't enjoy the meal (very) **much**.*
But in a positive sentence we do not
use *much* on its own.
 *I enjoyed the meal **very much**.*

D Some adverbs can modify a
preposition.
 *The office is **right in** the city centre.*
Some can modify a quantifier.
 ***Very few** people would agree.*
 *I've made **quite a lot of** mistakes.*

TIP

We use *not very* for a small degree or
a negative judgement. Say *The photos
aren't very good* rather than *They aren't
good* or *They're bad*.

128

Too, enough, quite, rather, and such

A *Too* comes before an adjective or adverb.
   *The water is **too cold** to swim in.*
   *Hang on. You're going **too fast**.*
   *This coat is much **too big** for me.*

   Enough follows an adjective or adverb.
   *The water isn't **warm enough** to swim in.*
   *I didn't react **quickly enough**.*

B We can use most adverbs of degree after *a/an*, e.g. *a very warm welcome* or *a fairly big crowd*. But we do not use *so* in this position. Instead, we use this pattern with *such*.
   *We received **such a warm** welcome.*
   (NOT ~~a so warm welcome~~)
   We use the same pattern with *quite*.
   *There was **quite a big** crowd.*
   A quite big crowd is less usual. But with *rather*, both patterns are possible.
   ***a rather big** crowd / **rather a big** crowd*

   We can also use *such/quite/rather* + *a/an* + noun without an adjective.
   *Don't make **such a fuss**.*
   *We had to wait **quite a while**.*
   *It's **rather a pity** we can't go.*

C *Too* or *as* + adjective go before *a/an*.
   *You've cut **too short a** piece.*
   *You don't get **as nice a** view from here.*

D *Quite* means 'fairly' when it comes
before a gradable adjective.
> *The task is **quite difficult**.*
> *The film was **quite good**.*

In British English, *quite* before an
ungradable adjective means 'completely'.
> *The task is **quite impossible**.*
> *The film was **quite brilliant**.*

Not quite means 'not completely'.
> *I'm **not quite** ready yet.*

Quite is not usually stressed.
> *It's quite* WARM *today.*

Here we focus on the warmth. But
when we stress *quite*, we limit the force
of the next word.
> *It's* QUITE *warm, but not* VERY *warm.*

E *Quite* and *rather* have a similar
meaning, but we tend to use *quite* for
favourable comments and *rather* for
unfavourable ones.
> *It was **quite a good** party, wasn't it?*
> *It was **rather a dull** party, wasn't it?*

Rather in a favourable comment often
means 'to a surprising degree'.
> *In fact the test paper was **rather easy**.*

TIP

You can use *quite* with a verb. *I quite
enjoyed the film* expresses a positive
opinion, although not as positive as *I
really enjoyed it*.

129

Focus, viewpoint, and truth adverbials

A *Only* and *even*

We can use *only* and *even* to focus on a word or phrase. We can put *only* before the relevant word or phrase.

*We're here for **only** two days.*
*I speak **only** a little French.*

Only can also be in mid position.

*We're **only** here for two days.*
*I **only** speak a little French.*

In official written English, *only* comes after the word or phrase focused on.

*Waiting limited to 30 minutes **only**.*
*Members **only*** (a notice)

Even goes in mid position or before the relevant word or phrase.

*Emma travels a lot. She's **even** been to the North Pole.*
*I never watch TV. I don't **even** own a set.*
*Jack always wears shorts, **even** in winter.*
*It was warm yesterday, and it's **even** warmer today.*

When we focus on the subject, we put *only* or *even* before it.

Only you *would do a silly thing like that.*
Even the experts *don't know the answer.*

B Viewpoint adverbials

These express the idea that we are looking at a situation from a particular aspect.

Financially, we've had a difficult year.

It's a good move for me *from a career point of view*.

As far as the weather is concerned, I'm not very optimistic.

These adverbials go in front or end position and can modify an adjective.

The plan is *environmentally* disastrous.

C Truth adverbials

These say how likely a statement is to be true, or in what way it is true.

Perhaps/Maybe it's a software problem.

We're *certainly/definitely* on course.

You've got satnav, *presumably*.

Clearly, the matter is urgent.

Most of these adverbs can go in front, mid, or end position. *Certainly*, *definitely*, and *probably* usually go in mid position. But we put a truth adverb before a negative auxiliary.

The company *basically* isn't interested.

We can also use a prepositional phrase.

In my opinion it's a great idea.

The results are good *on the whole*.

TIP

A clause with *I think*, *I expect*, etc has the same effect as a truth adverbial, e.g. *I think* it's a great idea.

---

130 Comment adverbials and linking adverbials

A We can use an adverb to comment on what is said in the rest of the sentence.

***Luckily** no one was killed.*

*The newspapers weren't interested in the story, **surprisingly**.*

***Unfortunately** we didn't win anything.*

These adverbs usually go in front or end position.

A clause with *I'm surprised, I'm afraid,* etc has the same effect.

***I'm surprised** they weren't interested.*

***I'm afraid** we didn't win anything.*

B We can also use an adverb to comment on someone's behaviour.

***Wisely**, the cashier obeyed the gunman.*

Mid position is also possible.

*The cashier **wisely** obeyed the gunman.*

C We can use a phrase with *to* for someone's reaction.

***To my surprise**, the place was deserted.*

*Chloe won a prize, **to her great delight**.*

D We can point out that we are being honest.

***Frankly**, I'm not interested in old cars.*

*I don't really have a choice, **to be honest**.*

***To tell the truth**, I'm against the idea.*

E Here are some ways of relating one clause to another using linking adverbials.

Adding something:	The baby grows bigger and heavier. Its shape **also** changes.
Expressing a contrast:	I know you don't believe me. **Nevertheless**, it's the truth.
Contradicting:	I expect you're tired. ~ **On the contrary**, I feel wide awake.
Correcting:	I'll see you tomorrow. **Or rather** on Monday.
Rephrasing:	It's under consideration. **In other words**, they're thinking about it.
Expressing a result:	We need to reduce costs, and **consequently** there will be job cuts.
Comparing:	I was tricked out of £50. Daniel was conned in **the same way**.
Ordering:	Of course the man is guilty. **Firstly**, he had a motive, and **secondly** his DNA was found on the victim.
Summing up:	**In conclusion**, I'd like to say a few words about future prospects.
Giving examples:	Colours affect us. Green, **for example**, is thought to be restful.
Changing the subject:	How can I help? This conversation is being recorded, **by the way**.
Supporting a statement:	I think I'd better be going. It's past midnight, **after all**.
Dismissing something:	I don't know if we did the right thing. **Anyway**, it doesn't matter now.

131 Comparison of adjectives

A Regular comparison

Short adjectives usually have a comparative form in *-er* and a superlative form in *-est*.

> It's **warmer** in here than outside.
> This is the **oldest** building in the town.

For spelling rules for *-er/-est*, ➤ 178A–B.

Long adjectives form the comparative and superlative with *more* and *most*.

> Skiing is **more difficult** than it looks.
> She's the **most irritating** person I know.

For more information on which adjectives have which form, ➤ B–D.

B One-syllable adjectives

Most one-syllable adjectives take *-er/-est*

> Our new flat is nicer.
> (NOT ~~Our new flat is more nice.~~)

Some take either *-er/-est* or *more/most*.

> I feel **safer / more safe** on the cycle path.

Such adjectives include: *clear, fair, free, keen, proud, rude, safe, sure, true*.

We use *more/most* (and not *-er/-est*) with *real, right, wrong* and with adjectives in *-ed*, e.g. *bored, pleased*.

> The story seemed **more real** in the film.
> Those **most pleased** to go were the kids.

C Two-syllable adjectives

Many of these take *more/most*.
> Our new place is **more central**.

These adjectives take *more/most*:

- Ending -*ful*, e.g. *careful, hopeful*
- Ending -*less*, e.g. *helpless, useless*
- Ending -*ing/-ed*, e.g. *boring, annoyed*
- Some others, e.g. *afraid, central, certain, complex, correct, exact, famous, foolish, frequent, modern, normal, recent.*

Some two-syllable adjectives take either -*er/-est* or *more/most*.
> Use the **simplest / most simple** method.

They include: *able, clever, common, cruel, feeble, gentle, narrow, pleasant, polite, quiet, simple, stupid, tired.*

We use -*er/-est* with most two-syllable adjectives ending in *y* (e.g. *angry, funny, happy*), although *more/most* is also possible.
> Life would be **easier** if I had a job.

D Three-syllable adjectives

Adjectives of three or more syllables take *more/most*.
> Your health is the **most important** thing.

TIP

If you are not sure about the correct form, it is safer to use *more/most*.

132 Irregular comparison and special forms

A The adjectives *good* and *bad* have irregular comparative and superlative forms:

* *good, better, best;*
* *bad, worse, worst.*

> Last week we saw a **good** game, but this week we saw an even **better** one. In fact it's the **best** I've seen for a long time. We've had **bad** weather for some time, and now it's getting **worse**. It's the **worst** of the winter so far.

For these forms used as adverbs, ➤ 133A.

B *Far* has two different comparative and superlative forms: *farther/further* and *farthest/furthest*.

> The **farthest/furthest** moon is 13 million kilometres from Saturn.

Further can mean 'more' or 'additional'.

> Let's hope there are no **further** problems. **Further** details on our website.

C *Elder, eldest* means the same as *older, oldest*. We use the irregular forms mainly to talk about ages in a family.

> Have you got an older/**elder** brother? Their oldest/**eldest** daughter married a Russian billionaire.

Elder and *eldest* go before the noun.

NOT *My brother is elder than me.*

D *Latest* and *last* mean different things.
Latest means 'furthest ahead in time'
or 'newest'.

> *What's the **latest** time we can leave and*
> *still get there on time?*
> *This jacket is the **latest** fashion.*
> (NOT ~~This jacket is the last fashion.~~)

Last means 'previous' or 'final'.
> *I had my hair cut **last** week.*
> (the week before this one)
> *The **last** bus goes at midnight.*
> (the final bus of the day)

E *Nearest* and *next* mean different
things. *Nearest* means 'the shortest
distance away'.

> *Where's the **nearest** post office?*
> (the one that is closest)

Next means 'following in a series'.
> *I'm going on holiday **next** week.*
> (the week after this one)
> *We have to get out at the **next** stop.*
> (the stop after this one)
> *There's a newsagent's in the **next** street.*
> (the street beside this one)

TIP

We can use *better* and *worse* as
comparative forms of *well* and *ill* to talk
about health and illness, e.g. *I expect
I'll be well again soon. I certainly feel
better than I did. I was much **worse**
yesterday.*

---

133 Comparison of adverbs and quantifiers

A Comparison of adverbs

Adverbs with the same form as adjectives (e.g. *hard* ➤ 123C) take *-er/-est*.
*You work **harder** than I do.*
*Who can shoot the **straightest**?*
*I got up **earlier** than usual.*

Well, *badly*, and *far* have irregular forms: *better, best*; *worse, worst*; and *farther, farthest* or *further, furthest*.
*I find these pills work **best**.*
*My tooth was aching **worse** than ever.*
*How much **farther/further** is it?*

Adverbs with *-ly* have *more/most*.
*You can draw **more accurately** than that.*
*The first speaker presented his case the **most convincingly**.*
But *early* is an exception (see above).

Adverbs not formed from adjectives (e.g. *often*) also have *more/most*.
*I wish we could meet **more often**.*
But *soon* is an exception.
*If I help, we'll finish the job **sooner**.*

Some adverbs have alternative forms, e.g. *cheap/cheaply* ➤ 123D. There is also a choice of comparative/superlative forms.
*You can buy them **cheaper** / **more cheaply** on the internet.*

B Comparison of quantifiers

Plural	*Uncountable*
more (a larger number)	more (a larger amount)
There are **more** cars in Los Angeles than people.	You've got **more** money than I have.
most (the largest number)	most (the largest amount)
AC Milan has the **most** points.	Claire is always studying. She does the **most** work.
fewer/less (a smaller number)	less (a smaller amount)
There are **fewer/less** phone boxes than there used to be.	If you want to be healthy, you should eat **less** fat.
fewest/least (the smallest number)	least (the smallest amount)
We're bottom of the league. We've got the **fewest/least** points.	I'm the busiest person here. I have the **least** spare time.

Some people think *less phone boxes* and *the least points* are incorrect, although they are commonly used.

134 Comparison: *than, as,* etc

A We often use *than* after a comparative.
*Glagow is bigger **than** Edinburgh.*
*Flying is a lot quicker **than** going by train.*
*Prices are higher **than** I expected.*

B *Less, least* are the opposites of *more, most.*
*The place is **less** busy on a Sunday.*
*This is the **least** expensive model.*
*I see Vicky **less** often these days.*
*My back hurts **less** if I lie down.*

C We use the pattern *as ... as ...* to say
that things are equal.
*The tree is **as** tall **as** the house.*
In a negative statement we use either
as ... as ... or *so ... as ... .*
*I don't drink **as/so** much tea **as** you do.*
*Watching sport on TV isn't **as/so**
exciting **as** being there.*
*The film isn't **as/so** good **as** the book.*
(The book is better.)

D These examples have an adverb of
degree before a comparative or *as.*
*France is **much** bigger than Belgium.*
*I'm feeling **a bit** less nervous now.*
*The holiday was **just** as good as the
brochure said it would be.*
We can also use *even* with a comparative.
*This stadium is pretty big, but the new
one will be **even** bigger.*

E This pattern with *and* expresses a
continuing change.
> *The plant grew **taller and taller**.*
> *The air gets **more and more polluted**.*
> *There's **more and more traffic**.*

With *more*, we do not repeat the adjective.
(NOT ~~more polluted and more polluted~~)

We can also use *less*.
> *I felt **less and less keen** on the idea.*

F A pattern with *the ... the ...* links a change
in one thing to a change in another.
> ***The further** you go, **the more** you pay.*
> ***The later** I get up, **the more tired** I feel.*
> ***The older** you get, **the harder** it
> becomes to start a new career.*

G After a superlative we often use a
phrase or a relative clause.
> *Which is the oldest city **in the world**?*
> *It's going to be the best gig **of all time**.*
> *That was the nicest meal **I've ever had**.*

We sometimes use *one of / some of*
before a superlative.
> *Turn left for **one of** the most magnificent
> views you'll ever see in your life.*

TIP

A pronoun on its own after *as* or *than*
has the object form, e.g. *I'm not as tall
as him*. It is formal and old-fashioned to
say *I'm not as tall **as he***. But we say *I'm
not as tall **as he is***.

269

135 Introduction to prepositions

A A preposition is a word like *in*, *to*, or *for*.
It usually comes before a noun phrase.
into the house **at** lunch **without** a coat
It can also be more than one word.
next to the window **on top of** the hill

Some prepositions can also come
before an adverb.
until tomorrow **through** there

B A phrase like *at the office* is a
prepositional phrase. It often functions
as an adverbial.
*We were very busy **at the office**.*
***On Tuesday** things were back to
normal.*
It can also come after a noun.
*The panic **at the office** was soon over.*

C Many idiomatic combinations have a
preposition following a verb, adjective,
or noun. ➤ 145–147
*wait **for** me keen **on** golf a tax **on** beer*

There are also many idiomatic phrases
beginning with a preposition.
***Above all**, we don't want any accidents.*
*You must let me know **at once**.*
*The house is **for sale**.*
***Of course** you can stay.*
***On the whole** we've had a good year.*

D We can use certain prepositions before a gerund. ➤ 75–76

*We succeeded **in moving** the piano.*

But we do not use a preposition + infinitive.

NOT ~~*We succeeded in to move the piano.*~~

And we do not use a preposition + that-clause.

NOT ~~*We're hoping for that it stays fine.*~~

We use one of these patterns.

We're hoping for fine weather.
We're hoping (that) it stays fine.

For a preposition + wh-clause, ➤ 163E.

*I'll make a list **of what** we need.*

E We can modify a preposition.

*   ***just off** the motorway*   ***all over** the floor*
*   ***almost at** the end*   ***halfway up** the hill*

F Sometimes a preposition goes at the end of a wh-question, a passive clause, an infinitive clause, or a relative clause.

*Who did you go out **with**?* ➤ 10E
*The matter has been looked **into**.* ➤ 59D
*There's plenty to think **about**.* ➤ 64D
*Here's the key I was looking **for**.* ➤ 172D

TIP

Many idiomatic phrases beginning with a preposition have a noun on its own without a determiner, e.g. *in fact, on average, on holiday, out of work, under pressure.*

136 Prepositions of place

A Some common prepositions

*There's a man **in/inside** the phone box.*
*You can park **outside** the bank.*
*Lunch is **on** the table.*
*There's a flag **on top of** the building.*
*The dog was **under(neath)** the table.*
*The clock is **over/above** the entrance.*
*Coming **down** the steps is easier than*
  *climbing **up** them.*
*The fans were going **in/into** the stadium.*
*Afterwards they came **out of** the stadium.*
*The road goes **through** a tunnel.*
*I tipped the money **on/onto** the counter.*
*Take those shoes **off** the table, please.*
*I was waiting **at** the traffic lights.*
*We took a train **from** Bath **to** Bristol.*
*We were driving **away from** the coast*
  *and **towards** the mountains.*
*I was sitting **next to** / **by** / **beside** Kylie.*
  *Our table was **close to** / **near** the door.*
*Nicola was first. She was **in front of** /*
  ***ahead of** me in the queue. Rebecca was*
  ***behind** me. I was **between** the two.*
*We walked **along** the pavement.*
*A car went **past** the school at high speed.*
*We walked **across** the road.*
*I smiled at the man sitting **opposite** me.*
*I lost my friend **among** the crowds.*
*The athletes run **(a)round** the track.*
*David was leaning **against** the wall.*
*The submarine is 500 metres **below** us.*
*Who knows what lies **beyond** those hills?*

B Position and movement

Most prepositions of place can express both position and movement.

*There was a barrier **across** the road.*
*A dog ran **across** the road.*

At usually expresses position, and *to* expresses movement.

*We were **at** the café.*
*We went **to** the café.*

As a general rule, *in* and *on* express position, and *into* and *onto* express movement.

*We were **in** the café / **on** the balcony.*
*He went **into** the café / **onto** the balcony.*

But in informal English we also use *in* and *on* for movement.

*We went **in** the café.*
*Babies often throw things **on** the floor.*

C Other meanings

Prepositions of place can also have more abstract meanings. For example:

*She's really **into** yoga.* (interested in)
*The talk is **on** China.* (about China)
*We're right **behind** you.* (supporting)

> **TIP**
>
> After *lay, place, put,* and *sit* we usually use *in* or *on* rather than *into* or *onto*, e.g. *They laid the body **on** a blanket. Advertisements were placed **in** the newspapers. She sat **on** the table.*

137 Place: *at*, *on*, and *in*

A We use *at* for position.
  *I was **at** the bus stop.*
  *There's someone **at** the door.*
  We see *the bus stop* and *the door* as a
  point in space.

  We use *at* with a building or
  institution when we mean its normal
  purpose.
  *She's **at** the theatre.* (watching a play)
  *I'm still **at** school.* (attending school)

  We use *at* with someone's house and
  with a social event.
  *We were all **at** Alice's (house/flat).*
  *We met **at** Adam's party, didn't we?*

B *On* is two-dimensional. We use it for a
  surface.
  *Don't leave your glasses **on** the floor.*
  *There were pictures **on** the walls.*
  We also use it for position on a line.
  *Bath is **on** the River Avon.*

C *In* is three-dimensional.
  *I had ten pounds **in** my pocket.*
  *Who's that girl **in** the green dress?*
  *We sat **in** the waiting room.*

  Compare *in* and *at* with buildings.
  *It was cold **in** the library.* (the building)
  *We were **at** the library.* (using it)

D In general we use *in* for a country or town.

> He's **in** Canada / **in** Birmingham.

With a small place we use *at* or *in*.

> We live **at/in** a place called Menston.

We can use *at* for a town or city as a point on a journey.

> We had to change trains **at** Brno.

E Compare these phrases.

> **at** 52 Church Street   **at** your house
> **at** this address   **at** the station
> **at** home/work/school   **at** the seaside
> **at** the back/end/front of the queue

> **on** 42nd Street (US)   **on** the third floor
> **on** the platform   **on** the screen
> **on** the island   **on** the right/left
> **on** the beach   **on** the coast   **on** the page
> **on** the back of an envelope

> **in** Spain   **in** Bristol   **in** Church Street
> **in** the room   **in** the lesson
> **in** a book/newspaper   **in** the middle
> **in** the picture/photo   **in** the country
> **in** the distance   **in** the back of the car
> **in** a queue/line/row

TIP

Use *on* with a small island and *in* with a large one, e.g. *We spent two weeks **on** Corfu / **in** Ireland.*

138 More on prepositions of place

A *Above, over, below, under*

Above and *over* have similar meanings.
*The flat is **over/above** the shop.*

We prefer *over*:

- when two things are in contact;
  *Someone spread a sheet **over** the body.*
- for movement to the other side;
  *The horse jumped **over** the wall.*
- with a number.
  *The crowd was **over** 20,000.*
  But we use *above* for a vertical
  measurement.
  *Temperatures will rise **above** 30°.*

Below is the opposite of *above*.
*The pipe was two metres **below** ground.*
Under is the opposite of *over*.
*Come **under** the umbrella.*
Under is more usual with numbers.
*The winner gets just **under** £2 million.*

B *Through, across, along*

You go *through* a tunnel, forest, hole,
etc.
*The burglar got in **through** a window.*

You go *across* a road, bridge, frontier, etc.
*You can get **across** the river by ferry.*

You go *along* a path, road, coast, etc.
*Someone was coming **along** the
corridor.*

C Near, close, by, next to

Near (to) and *close to* me   from'.

There's a taxi rank **near**
Don't put a heater **close**

Nearby / close by means 'not
There are excellent restaurants **n.**

By means 'at the side of' or 'very ne
We live **by** the school. Sit **by** me.

Next to means 'directly at the side of'.
They parked **next to** us. Sit **next to** me.

D In front of, behind

For place we prefer *in front of* to *before*.
There's a statue **in front of** the museum.
And we prefer *behind* to *after*.
The car **behind** us ran into us.

E Between, among

We use *between* with a small number
of separate things, especially two
things.
The ball went **between** the player's legs.
Among suggests a larger number.
I saw someone **among** the trees.
Among the crowd was my uncle.

TIP

Do not confuse *in front of* and *opposite*.
Compare *He sat **in front of** me in the
cinema* and *He sat **opposite** me at
lunch*.

: *at*, *on*, and *in*

√e use *at* for a particular time, e.g. a clock time, a meal time, or a short holiday period.

*The match starts **at** three o'clock.*
*I'll see you **at** breakfast*
*What are you doing **at** Christmas?*
*We're away **at** the weekend.*
(US: ***on** the weekend*)
*We're very busy **at** the moment.*
***At** that time there was no internet.*

B We use *on* with a day.
*The meeting is **on** Tuesday / **on** 8 May.*
*I won't be here **on** that day.*
*What happens **on** Independence Day?*

C We use *in* with longer periods.
*I have to decide **in** the next few days.*
*It's busy here **in** the summer holidays.*
*The term starts **in** September.*
*The company was set up **in** 1997.*
*The church was built **in** the 13th century.*

We also use *in* with part of a day.
*I always work better **in** the afternoon.*
But we use *on* if we say which day.
*Why not come over **on** Friday afternoon?*
*The incident occurred **on** the evening of 27 April.*

D We use *in* for how long something takes.
   *Can you run a mile **in** four minutes?*

We can also use *in* for a time in the future measured from the present.
   *We'll take our exams **in** three weeks.*

Compare these examples.
   *You can walk there **in** half an hour.*
   (It takes half an hour.)
   *I'm going out **in** half an hour.*
   (half an hour from now)

E Sometimes we use an expression of time without a preposition.
   *I received the letter **last Thursday**.*
   *I'm starting a new course **next year**.*
   *The same thing happens **every time**.*
   *I'll see you **tomorrow morning**.*
   *A **week later** I got a reply.*
We do not normally use *at*, *on*, or *in* with *last*, *next*, or *this*; with *every* or *all*; with *yesterday* or *tomorrow*; or with the adverb *later*.

In some contexts we can either use the preposition or leave it out.
   *I was feeling unwell (**on**) that day.*
   *Profits were higher (**in**) the previous year.*
   *We met (**on**) the following Monday.*

TIP

In informal English, and especially in American English, *on* is often left out in e.g. *I'll see you **Monday***.

279

140 *For, since,* and *ago*

A We use *for* with a period of time to say how long something continues.

> *I can surf the internet **for** hours on end.*
> *I once stayed at that hotel **for** a week.*
> *Let's just sit down **for** five minutes.*

We do not use *for* before *all* + noun.

> *It rained **all day**.* (NOT *for all day*)

And we do not usually use *for* before a phrase with *whole*.

> *It rained **the whole day**.*

This is more usual than *for the whole day*.

B We often use *for* and *since* with the perfect. We use *for* + length of time.

> *I've worked there **for** five years now.*
> *We haven't seen Rory **for** months.*
> *I've been waiting here **for** twenty minutes.*

We can sometimes leave out *for* in informal English.

> *I've been waiting twenty minutes.*

We use *since* + time when.

> *I've worked here **since** 2005.*
> *We haven't seen Rory **since** August.*
> *I've been waiting here **since** twelve o'clock.*

We sometimes also use *since* with an event.

> *I haven't been out **since** the concert.*

C We use the adverb *ago* for something that happened at a time in the past measured from the present.

> *I joined the company five years **ago**.*
> *We last saw Rory months **ago**.*
> *An hour **ago** I was still in bed.*

Ago comes after the length of time (*five years, months, an hour*).

When we look back to an even earlier time, we usually use the adverb *before*.

> *Rachel left the company last year. She'd joined them five years **before**.*

This is more usual than *She'd joined them five years ago.*

D Compare these examples.

Looking into the past:

> *I've been here (**for**) ten minutes.*
> *I've been here **since** four forty.*
> *I arrived ten minutes **ago**.*

Looking into the future:

> *I'll stay (**for**) ten minutes.*
> *I'll stay **until** five o'clock.*
> *I'm leaving **in** ten minutes.*

TIP

Don't use *since* with a phrase expressing length of time. Say **for** *four days* but **since** *Tuesday*, **for** *two years* but **since** *2008*. A useful sentence when you meet someone after a long time is *I haven't seen you **for** ages.*

141 More prepositions of time

A Place and time

Some prepositions of place can also be used with time.

*I'll be there **between** three and half past.*
*You can do the journey **inside** an hour.*

At, *on*, and *in* can also express either place ➤ 137 or time ➤ 139.

B *During*

We use *during* with an event or a specific period of time.

*Nobody works **during** the festival.*
*I suddenly felt ill **during** the meeting.*
*The office will be closed **during** August.*
*I have to be away several times **during** the next couple of months.*

We do not use *during* + length of time.

*The festival went on **for** five days.*
(NOT *It went on during five days.*)

During is a preposition; *while* is a conjunction.

*I fell asleep **during** the film.*
*I fell asleep **while** I was watching the film.*

C *Till/until* and *by*

We use *till/until* to say when something comes to an end.

*We stayed **till/until** the end of the show.*
*I'll be working here **till/until** next April.*

Till is more informal than *until*.
Not ... till/until means that something
happens later than expected.
  We did**n't** arrive **till** one in the
  morning.
  We won**'t** get the money **until** next year.

By means 'not later than'.
  I have to be at work **by** nine.
  They should have replied **by** now.
  By the time I got home, I was exhausted.
  She's going to pay me back **by** Friday.
  (on Friday or earlier)
But *before Friday* means 'earlier than
Friday'.

D *From ... to/till/until*

We use *from* for the time something
starts.
  Tickets will be on sale **from** tomorrow.
  From 6 a.m. there's the noise of traffic.

For starting and finishing times we use
from ... to or *from ... till/until*.
  The season is **from** April **to** September.
  The road will be closed **from** Friday
  evening **until** Monday morning.
Americans use *through*, e.g. *from
Friday **through** Monday*.

TIP

Do not use *till/until* for place.
Say We walked **as far as** the bridge,
not ~~until the bridge~~.

283

142

Prepositions: other meanings

A Here are some examples of prepositions with meanings other than place or time.

*We were arguing **about** politics.*
*I'm reading a book **by** Julian Barnes.*
*The voters were **in favour of** the idea.*
*Can I use a pencil **instead of** a pen?*
*It's **up to** you whether you accept or not.*

B Here are some uses of *for*.

*Could you do something **for** me, please?*
*I just called in **for** a chat.* (purpose)
*Are you **for** or against the idea?*

C Here are some uses of *with*.

*I went to the concert **with** a friend.*
*Matt is the man **with** long hair.*
*I cut the wood **with** an electric saw.*
*He shouted **with** fury.* (furiously)
***With** her watching, I felt nervous.* ➤ 82B

D To talk about an instrument, we use *with*.

*They broke the lock **with** a hammer.*
*Just stir this **with** a wooden spoon.*

We use *by* before an ing-form.

*They got in **by** breaking the lock.*

We use *by* + agent with the passive.

*The lock was broken **by** the thieves.*
*The motor is powered **by** electricity.*

E We use *by* + noun for means of transport.
*I prefer to travel **by** train.*
We can say *by air, by bike, by taxi*, etc.

But *by* is not used for a specific vehicle.
*I'll go **in my car**. (NOT ~~I'll go by my car.~~)*
We can say *in the/my car, in a taxi, on the bus/ferry/train*, etc, and *on foot. By foot* is also possible.

We also use *by* for means of communication, e.g. *by fax, by email.*
*I sent the information **by** post.*

F *As* can express a role or function.
*I'm using the sofa **as** a bed.*
*Maria has come **as** our guide.*
(She is our guide.)

We use *like* to make a comparison.
*My brother can swim **like** a fish.*
*You look a bit **like** Brad Pitt.*

Compare *as* and *like*.
*He speaks **as** an expert. He is after all a professor.*
*He talks **like** an expert, but really he knows very little.*

TIP

Of is used in several different patterns,
e.g. *the end of the game* ➤ 86C, *a tin of soup* ➤ 88C, *some of my friends* ➤ 104C,
a sight of land ➤ 164.

143

Phrasal and prepositional verbs

A A phrasal verb is a verb + adverb.
Come in and *sit down*.
I *took off* my shoes.

A prepositional verb is a verb + preposition.
I was *looking at* the photo.
We didn't *go into* all the details.
The preposition has an object (*the photo*, *the details*).

B Some phrasal verbs have no object.
Suddenly the lights *went out*.
Others have an object.
Someone *turned out* the lights.

When a phrasal verb has an object, both these orders are usually possible.
We *woke up* the neighbours.
We *woke* the neighbours *up*.
The adverb (*up*) can go before or after the object (*the neighbours*).

When the object is a pronoun, the adverb goes after it.
The neighbours were annoyed because we *woke them up*.
When the object is a long phrase, the adverb usually goes before it.
We *woke up* just about everybody in the whole street.

C The adverb can sometimes go in front position for extra emphasis.

*The door opened, and **out** ran the boys.*

There is usually inversion of subject and verb, unless the subject is a pronoun.

*The door opened, and **out** they ran.*

D A prepositional verb always has an object after the preposition.

*Lisa paid **for the meal**. Lisa paid **for it**.*

Compare these examples.

*She **looked at** it.*

(prepositional verb – stress on *looked*)

*She **put** it **away**.*

(phrasal verb – stress on *away*)

E An adverbial usually goes after the phrasal verb but between a verb and preposition.

*The plane took off **on time**.*

*I looked **carefully** at the photo.*

F Many phrasal and prepositional verbs can be passive.

*The alarm has been **switched off**.*

*The matter will be **dealt with**.*

TIP

Some verb + adverb combinations can be used as a noun, e.g. a **handout** for each student, a **hold-up** at the bank, a car **breakdown**, an hour before **take-off**.

287

144 Phrasal verb meanings

A Some phrasal verbs are easy to understand if you know the meaning of each word.

*You can **turn round** here and **go back**.*

But often the phrasal verb has an idiomatic meaning.

*I've **given up** smoking.* (stopped)
*Will the idea **catch on**?* (become popular)

B Some one-word verbs have the same meaning as a phrasal verb. The phrasal verb is usually more informal.

*Try to **find out**/discover the reason.*
*We must **fix up**/arrange a meeting.*
*They've **put off**/postponed the match.*

Others include: *carry on/continue, keep up/maintain, leave out/omit, put up/raise, take away/remove.*

C Some verbs combine with different adverbs.

*The child took two steps and **fell down**.*
*Chloe and I have **fallen out**.* (quarrelled)
*The deal **fell through**.* (didn't happen)

And the most common adverbs can combine with many different verbs.

*Prices may **come down** soon.*
*A girl was **knocked down** by a car.*
*The factory has **closed down**.*
*Could you **turn** the radio **down**?*

D A phrasal verb can have more than one
meaning.
> *There wasn't room to **get by**.* (go past)
> *I'm not rich, but I **get by**.* (manage to live)

E We can use an adverb with *be*.
> *I'll be **away** next week.* (not here)
> *Will you be **in** tomorrow?* (at home/work)
> *The wedding is **off**.* (not taking place)
> *The party's **over**.* (at an end)

F Here are some adverbs often used in
phrasal verbs.
> *down* = to the ground: *fell **down***
> *down* = on paper: *write **down** the number*
> *down* = becoming less: *slow **down***
> *off* = away: *set **off** on a journey*
> *off* = disconnected: *turn **off** the TV*
> *on* = wearing: *put my shoes **on***
> *on* = connected: *switch the light **on***
> *on* = continuing: *keep **on** walking*
> *out* = away/disappearing: *put **out** a fire*
> *out* = to different people: *hand **out** copies*
> *out* = aloud: *read **out** a poem*
> *over* = from start to finish: *check it **over***
> *up* = increasing: *step **up** production*
> *up* = completely: *use **up** all the paper*

TIP

You do not have to learn each phrasal
verb separately. If you know that *down*
can mean 'to the ground', you can guess
the meaning of *knock down the houses*
and *cut down a tree*.

---

145 Prepositional verbs

A A prepositional verb is a verb +
preposition combination.

*I can't **concentrate on** my work.*
*The flat **consists of** four rooms.*
*What does this number **refer to**?*

Which preposition goes after the verb
is mainly a matter of idiom.

For a comparison of prepositional
verbs and phrasal verbs, ➤ 143.

B Some verbs can take a number
of different prepositions. Each
combination has a different meaning.

*I have to **look after** the baby.*
*Come and **look at** the view.*
*I'm **looking for** my mobile.*
*The police are **looking into** the incident.*
*We're going to **look round** the shops.*

C We can use *about* after many different
verbs expressing speech or thought.

*We were **talking about** renting a flat.*
*We'll have to **decide about** our holiday.*

Compare *ask about* and *ask for*.

*We **asked about** cheap tickets.*
('Please tell us about cheap tickets.')
*We **asked for** cheap tickets.*
('Please give us cheap tickets.')

D We usually use *to* before the person we are addressing.

> We were **talking to**/with our friends.
> We **complained to** the manager.

But we say *laugh at, smile at, argue with,* and *communicate with.*

> Everyone **laughed at** the clown.
> Are you **arguing with** me?

We *ring, (tele)phone, call,* or *mail* a person. We do not use *to.*

> I **phoned** my boss.

E Some verbs have a similar meaning to a prepositional verb but take a direct object.

> The troops have **entered** the city.
> (NOT ~~entered into the city~~)
> We were **discussing** politics.
> (NOT ~~discussing about politics~~)

Others include: *accompany, answer, approach, control, demand, lack, marry, obey, reach, remember, resemble, seek, suit.*

The equivalent noun takes a preposition.

> their **entry into** the city
> a **discussion about** politics

TIP

Some verbs can take either an object or a preposition, depending on the meaning, e.g. *I **paid** the bill* but *I **paid for** the meal.* Also *approve (of), leave (for), search (for).*

146

Prepositional verbs: more complex patterns

A Some prepositional verbs have an object between the verb and preposition.

*Can you **translate the text into** English?*
*I must **thank Daniel for** helping us.*
*We **spend too much money on** clothes.*
*I **prefer wine to** beer.*

Others include *compare ... with, congratulate ... on, criticize ... for, insure ... against, turn ... into.*

In the passive, the preposition comes directly after the verb.

*The article was **translated into** English.*
*Too much money is **spent on** clothes.*

B Compare these pairs of sentences.

*You can't **blame** me **for** everything.*
*You can't **blame** everything **on** me.*
*We **provide** our guests **with** security.*
*We **provide** security **for** our guests.*

C We use *about* after *tell/ask* + object.

*Did I **tell** you **about** my new job?*
*We **asked** our friends **about** their plans.*

We can ask someone *for* something.

*We **asked** our friends **for** some help.*

After *inform* and *warn* we can use *about* or *of*.

*We will **inform/warn** customers **about/ of** any changes to these arrangements.*

PREPOSITIONAL VERBS: PATTERNS

With *communicate*, *describe*, *explain*,
and *write*, we use *to* before the person
receiving the message.

> He **communicated** the news **to** them.
> Can you **describe** the man **to** me?

D Sometimes a verb + object + preposition
can have an idiomatic meaning.

> Nurses **take care of** the patients.
> Let's **make the most of** this weather.
> Should we **put our faith in** alternative
> medicine?

E A verb can have both an adverb and a
preposition after it.

> The room **looks out over** fields.
> The astronomer **gazed up at** the stars.

These are 'phrasal-prepositional verbs'.
Sometimes the meaning is idiomatic.

> I need to **cut down on** fatty food.
> You've got to **face up to** the situation.
> I must **get round to** these little jobs.

There can be an object after the verb.

> Don't **let anyone in on** our secret.
> I might **take you up on** that invitation.

TIP

Some idioms consist of a verb and a
prepositional phrase, e.g. *We took all
the facts into consideration.* Others
include: *throw ... into a panic, drive ...
to distraction, put ... out of action.*

147 Adjective/Noun + preposition

A Some adjectives can be followed by a preposition.

*The place was **crowded with** tourists.*
*The town is **famous for** its market.*
*He was found **guilty of** burglary.*
*You'll be **late for** work.*
*This flat is **similar to** ours.*
*That remark is **typical of** a man.*

Many of these adjectives express feelings.

afraid of the dark   **eager for** news
fed up with housework   **keen on** fishing
thrilled at/by the idea

B Some adjectives can take different prepositions depending on the meaning.

*We were **anxious about** terrorists.*
*Everyone was **anxious for** news.*

C We use *good at*, etc to talk about ability.

*Mike is **good at** skating.*
*You're **brilliant at** maths.*
*I'm **bad at / hopeless at** any sport.*

We use *at* with an activity and *with* to talk about other things.

*I'm no good **at** budgeting / **with** money.*

We use *good for / bad for* to say if something benefits you or not.

*Regular exercise is **good for** you.*
*Too much sugar is **bad for** anyone.*

For behaviour towards someone, we use *good to*, *rude to*, etc.

> You've been very **good to / kind to** me.
> The waiter was barely **polite to** us.

D Some nouns can be followed by a preposition.

> There's a good **chance of** fine weather.
> This is the **key to** the whole problem.
> What's the **reason for** this decision?
> They've increased the **tax on** petrol.
> I'm having **trouble with** the computer.
> It was a **talk about/on** recycling.

Some nouns to do with needs and desires are followed by *for*.

> There is a **need for** more housing.
> Is there any **demand for** these products?

Others include: *an appetite for, an application for, a demand for, a desire for, a request for, a taste for, a wish for.*

Compare the use of *with* and *between*.

> There is a **link with** another murder.
> There is a **link between** the two murders.

Also: *connection, contrast, relationship.*

TIP

If you know what preposition comes after a related verb or adjective, this may help. We say **invited to** the party and an **invitation to** the party; **afraid of** flying and a **fear of** flying. But sometimes the preposition is different, e.g. *proud* **of** his victory but *pride* **in** his victory.

---

148 Clause and sentence

A Main clauses

A main clause is one that can stand
alone as a sentence. ➤ 2

A woman went into a shop.

We can use *and*, *or*, *but*, and *so* to join
main clauses. ➤ 150–151

*She put a sweater in her bag, **and** she
walked out of the store.*

*She tried to run **but** she was caught.*

When the subject of the two clauses
is the same, we can often leave it out,
especially after *and* and *or*.

*She put it in her bag **and walked** out.*

B Sub-clauses

A sub-clause cannot stand alone.

*The alarm rang **as she left the store**.*

*She knew **that she was in trouble**.*

Here *as she left the store* and *that she
was in trouble* are sub-clauses, not
complete sentences. The word order is
the same as in a main clause.

NOT *She knew that she in trouble was.*

C Finite/non-finite clauses

A non-finite clause has an infinitive,
a gerund, or a participle.

*The manager decided **to ring the police**.*

*She admitted **stealing the sweater**.*

***Hearing the alarm**, she started to run.*

Non-finite verbs often have no subject, but they can sometimes have one.

__Her heart racing__, she walked to the door.

A main clause is always finite.

The manager __rang__ the police.

A sub-clause can be finite or non-finite.

Finite: *She decided __she would steal__ it.*

Non-finite: *She decided __to steal__ it.*

D Clause combinations

In speech you may hear a number of main clauses linked by *and*.

She put the sweater in her bag __and__ went out, __and__ the alarm rang, __and__ a security man ran after her.

Sub-clauses are also used in speech.

I became a policeman __when I was 29__, and I've enjoyed it __because every day is interesting__.

This written sentence has a main clause, relative clause, two infinitive clauses, an adverbial clause, and a that-clause.

Japan, which has no fossil fuel reserves, wants to stockpile plutonium because it believes that it can develop the technology to transform it into cheap electricity.

TIP

Don't be afraid of the word *and*. You can even use it to begin a sentence, especially in conversation.

What comes after the verb?

A Here are some common patterns with a verb + sub-clause.

That-clause	I know **(that)** you're busy.
Object + that-clause	He promised **us (that)** he wouldn't be late.
Wh-clause	I can't remember **who** told me the news.
Object + wh-clause ➤ 70C	Tell **me what** you've been doing.
Question word + to-infinitive ➤ 70C	Have you decided **where to go?**
Object + question word + to-infinitive ➤ 70C	No one taught **me how to cook** properly.
To-infinitive ➤ 66	We're aiming **to be** back by five.
Object + to-infinitive ➤ 68	I want **you to keep** still.
For + object + to-infinitive ➤ 71	I've arranged **for my mail to be** sent on.
Object + infinitive without *to* ➤ 72D	This show always makes **me laugh.**
Gerund ➤ 66A, 66C	I suggested **waiting** a bit longer.
Object + gerund ➤ 74D	They've stopped **people parking** here.
Preposition + gerund ➤ 76A	I used to dream **of going** on the stage.

B Here are some examples of verbs and their patterns.

accept that it is • **accuse** me of doing • **admit** (that) you did it / having done it • **advise** me to do it / (me) what to do / (me) against doing it • **agree** that it is / to do it • **aim** to do it • **allow** me to do it • **apologize** (to me) for doing it • **arrange** that it will happen / (for me) to do it • **assume** (that) it is • **avoid** doing it • **believe** (that) it is / in doing it • **cause** it to happen • **choose** to do it • **consider** (that) it is / what is happening / it to be so / doing it • **decide** (that) I will do it / what I'll do / to do it / what to do • **demand** (that) I do it / to do it • **deny** (that) it is so / doing it / having done it • **doubt** (that) it is / if it is / whether it is • **dream** (that) it happened / of doing it • **expect** (that) it will be / (me) to do it • **explain** (that) it is / what happened • **force** me to do it • **help** (to) do it / me (to) do it • **hope** (that) it is / to do it • **insist** (that) it is / on doing it • **intend** to do it / doing it • **invite** me to go • **involve** doing it • **know** (that) it is / what happens • **learn** (how) to do it • **let** me do it • **like** (me) doing it / (me) to do it / it when I do • **make** me do it • **don't mind** what happens / (me) doing it / if it is • **need** to do it • **object** (that) it is / to (me) doing it • **offer** to do it • **permit** me to do it • **persuade** me to do it • **predict** (that) it will / what will happen • **prefer** to do it • **pretend** (that) it is / to do it • **prevent** me (from) doing it • **promise** (that) it will / me (that) it will / to do it • **propose** (that) it should be / doing it / to do it • **refuse** to do it • **remind** me (that) it is / me what happens / me to do it • **require** me to do it • **show** me (that) it is / (that) it is / (me) what happens / me to be • **stop** doing it / me (from) doing it • **succeed** in doing it • **suggest** (that) it should / doing it • **suppose** (that) it is / it to be • **teach** (me) (how) to do it • **understand** (that) it is / what happens • **want** (me) to do it • **warn** (that) it might / me (that) it might / me not to do it / me against doing it • **wish** (that) it would / to do it • **wonder** why it is / if it will / whether it will

299

150 Words meaning *and* and *or*

A We can use *and* to link two clauses.
> *I've seen the film, **and** I've read the book.*

Too/as well/also are more emphatic.
> *Shakespeare wrote plays, and he was an actor **too / as well**.*
> *He wrote plays. He was **also** an actor.*

B With a negative we use *either*, not *too*.
> *I haven't seen the film, and I haven't read the book **either**.*

And we often use *or* rather than *and*.
> *I haven't seen the film **or** read the book.*
> *I didn't have a coat **or** an umbrella.*

C We can use *besides* and *what's more* to make an extra point.
> *I'm too tired to go for a walk. **Besides**, it looks like rain.*
> *It's dangerous to phone while driving. **What's more**, it's against the law.*

Furthermore, moreover, and in addition are more typical of written English.
> *Some people have no car. **Furthermore**, there is little public transport.*
> *Students must sit three exam papers, and **in addition** there is a practical test.*

D We can use the prepositions *as well as*, *in addition to*, and *besides*.
> *He was an actor **as well as** a writer.*
> ***Besides** the rent, I have to pay for gas.*

E We use *or* to express an alternative.
  *I'd like to study at Oxford **or**
  Cambridge.*
  *We can take a bus, **or** (alternatively) we
  can walk.*

  Either ... or is more emphatic.
  *You'll have to go **either** right **or** left.*
  ***Either** we pay someone to do the job, **or**
  we do it ourselves.*

F *Or* can mean 'if not'. We can also use *or
  else* or *otherwise*.
  *We must go now, **or** (**else**) we'll be late.*
  *Put the leaflet in your bag, **otherwise**
  you'll lose it.*

G With two things, we can use *both ...
  and ...* for extra emphasis.
  *He was **both** a writer **and** an actor.*
  (NOT ~~He was and a writer and an actor.~~)

  Neither ... nor is more emphatic and
  can be a little formal.
  *I had **neither** a coat **nor** an umbrella.*
  ***Neither** Steve **nor** Amy was/were there.*
  *The old man can **neither** read **nor** write.*
  We use a positive verb, e.g. *can*.

TIP

As well as *both ... and ...*, we can use
not only ... but also ..., e.g. *He was **not
only** a writer **but also** an actor.*

---

151 Words meaning *but* and *so*

A We use *but* to express a contrast.
   *Julie is 20, **but** she looks younger.*
   We can also use the adverb *though*.
   *Julie is 20. She looks younger, **though**.*
   Tourism can bring benefits. On the whole,
   ***though**, its long-term impact is negative.*

   We sometimes use the conjunction *yet*
   in front position.
   *It was sunny, **yet** people were indoors.*

B The adverbs *however* and *nevertheless*
   are a little formal.
   *It was Sunday. **However/Nevertheless**,*
   the streets seemed as busy as usual.

   We can also use *even so* and *all the same*.
   *She had lots of friends. **Even so/All the***
   ***same**, she often felt lonely.*

C We can use the conjunction *although*,
   sometimes shortened to *though*.
   *I was angry, **though** I tried to hide it.*
   ***Although** Julie is 20, she looks younger.*

   Even though is more emphatic.
   *He didn't have a coat on, **even though***
   it was freezing. (NOT *even although*)

D We can use the prepositions *despite*
   and *in spite of*.
   *The game went ahead **despite** the rain.*
   *We got there **in spite of** losing the way.*

We can use *the fact that* + finite clause.
*The game went ahead despite / in spite of **the fact that** it was raining.*

E We use *whereas* or *while* for a comparison rather than a conflict between two ideas.
*I'm right-handed, **whereas/while** my brother is left-handed.*

F We use the conjunction *so* to express result.
*It hasn't rained, **so** the ground is very dry.*
We can use the adverbials *as a result*, *consequently*, and *therefore*.
*More women are working. **As a result** / **Consequently**, the birth rate is falling.*
*There has been little rainfall. The ground is **therefore** very dry.*

G This pattern with *so* or *such* and a that-clause expresses result.
*It's **so** dry (**that**) the plants are dying.*
*The place looked **such** a mess (**that**) I couldn't ask anyone in.*

TIP

Words meaning *but* can be conjunctions, prepositions, or adverbs. Each word class is used in a different grammatical pattern, e.g. *Although I felt tired ...*, *Despite feeling tired ...*, *I felt tired. However, ...*

152 Clauses of time

A Conjunctions of time

A clause of time often begins with a conjunction.

After we'd finished, we all had a rest.
Think carefully *before* you decide.
I've changed my job *since* I last saw you.
Jack could swim *when* he was a baby.

Others include: *as, as soon as, once, till/until, whenever, while.*

B Non-finite clauses of time

We can use a gerund with *after, before, on,* and *since.*

Think carefully *before deciding.*

We can use a participle after *once, until, when, whenever,* and *while.*

Take care *when crossing* the road.
Please wait *until told* to proceed.

We can also use a participle without a conjunction. ➤ 82A

Take care *crossing* the road.

C *When, while,* and *as*

We use these words for things happening at the same time. *While* and *as* suggest something continuing.

The model sat still *while* we drew her.
As I was cycling along, I saw a fox.

But for a time in your life, use *when.*

I'll be a millionaire *when* I'm thirty.

We also use *when* with two short
actions one after the other.
> **When** *I clicked the icon, everything froze.*

When can also mean 'every time'.
> *I cycle to work* **when/whenever** *it's fine.*

We can use *as* (not *while*) to say that
one change goes with another.
> *The mixture hardens* **as** *it cools.*

D *As soon as*, etc

As soon as means that one thing comes
immediately after another.
> **As soon as** *the gates were open, the
crowds rushed in.*

We can use these patterns with *no
sooner* and *hardly* with a similar
meaning to *as soon as*.
> *Emma was* **no sooner** *in bed* **than** *the
phone rang.*
> *I had* **hardly** *started work* **when** *I felt a
pain in my back.*

We can also use inversion.
> **No sooner** *was Emma in bed* **than** *...*
> **Hardly** *had I started work* **when** *...*

TIP

Do not use *by* as a conjunction. Use *by
the time*, e.g. *It was midday* **by the time**
I got to the office, not ~~It was midday by
I got to the office.~~

305

153 Reason and purpose

A Clauses of reason

We can form a clause of reason with a conjunction such as *because*.

*I made a mistake **because** I was tired.*

***As** it's so warm, I turned off the heating.*

***Since** we've started, let's carry on.*

***Seeing** it's so late, why not stay here?*

For meaning 'because' is rather literary.

*The cause of the accident is unclear, **for** there are many factors involved.*

We can use a participle clause. ➤ 82B

***Being** tired, I made a mistake.*

***Having spent** all the money, I couldn't pay the hotel bill.*

We can also use a preposition.

*The project was abandoned **because of** the cost.*

*The show was cancelled **due to** illness.*

***In view of** the risks, I would advise you not to take part.*

We also use *on account of* and *owing to*.

We can use *due to* and *in view of* with the fact that.

*The applicant was rejected **due to the fact that** he was not properly qualified.*

Out of can express motive.

*I had a look just **out of** curiosity.*

B Clauses of purpose

For purpose, we often use a to-infinitive.

*I went out **to buy** a newspaper.*
*You need a drill **to make** the holes.* ➤ 65C

In order to and *so as to* are more emphatic and a little formal.

*I arrived early **in order to** get a seat.*
*You can pay in instalments **so as to** spread the cost.*

The negative is *in order not to* or *so as not to*. *Not to* on its own is not possible.

*Allow lots of time **in order not to** be late.*
(NOT *Allow lots of time not to be late.*)

We can use a finite clause with *so that*.

*I recorded it **so that** I could watch it later.*

In informal style we can leave out *that*.

*I recorded it **so** I could watch it later.*

In order that is more formal than *so that*.

*You will receive full details **in order that** you may make your arrangements.*

We sometimes use *to avoid / to prevent* instead of a negative clause.

*I held it tight **so that** I wouldn't drop it.*
*I held it tight **to avoid** dropping it.*

TIP

We can use *for* + noun phrase to express the purpose of an action, e.g. *We went out **for** some fresh air.* And we use *for* + gerund to give the general purpose of something, e.g. *This paper is **for printing** photos on.*

154 *As* and *like*; *whoever*, etc

A *As* and *like*

We can use *as* and *like* as conjunctions.

*I kept quiet, **as/like** I was told to do.*

In more formal English, and especially in British English, *as* is preferred to *like*.

*The event was a great success, **as** it had been the previous year.*

But the equivalent preposition is *like* rather than *as*.

*It was just **like** the previous year.*

For the prepositions *as* and *like*, ➤ 142F.

We can use a clause with *as* when what we say is already known or expected.

***As** you know, I'll be leaving soon.*

*I was terrified, **as** you can imagine.*

We do not usually use *like* in this kind of clause, except informally with *say*.

***As/Like** I said, you're welcome to stay.*

B *As if* and *as though*

We can use these conjunctions to say how something seems.

*It was **as if** / **as though** I was dreaming.*

*It looks **as if** / **as though** it's going to be a nice day.*

*It feels **as if** / **as though** we're travelling quite slowly.*

The verbs *be*, *look*, *feel*, and *seem* are often used before *as if* / *as though*.

We can use *like* (informal) instead of
as if / *as though*.
  *It was **like** I was dreaming.*

We can also use *like* + ing-form.
  *It looks **like being** a nice day.*

C *Whoever, whatever,* etc

We can use *whoever, whatever,
whichever, whenever, wherever,* and
however meaning 'it doesn't matter
who, what', etc.

  ***Whoever** we elect, they won't have the
  power to change anything.*
  *I won't agree, **whatever** you say.*
  *It takes ages, **whichever** way you go.*
  *I can't draw, **however** hard I try.*

We can also use *no matter.*
  *I won't agree, **no matter** what you say.*

D *Whether ... or ...*

This means 'it doesn't matter if ... or ...' .
  ***Whether** the Conservatives **or** Labour
  win the election, it makes no difference.*
  *You have to pay in advance, **whether**
  you like it **or** not.*

TIP

You can use *feel like* + gerund to make
an informal suggestion, e.g. ***Do you
feel like going** to the cinema? ~ I don't
mind. What's on?*

155 Introduction to conditionals

A Most conditional sentences have a clause starting with *if*.

> **If** you haven't got TV, you can't watch it.
> We can sit down **if** we want to.
> **If** I phone the Helpline, they might be able to give me the information.
> **If** you lived on the planet Mercury, you'd have four birthdays in an Earth year.

We can use many different verb forms in conditional sentences. In an open condition (when something may or may not happen), we use the present tense (*If I phone ...*). For something unreal we often use the past tense (*If you lived ...*).

B There are some verb forms which often go together. These patterns are usually called Types 1, 2, and 3.

Type 1: *If the company **fails**, we **will lose** all our money.* ➤ 156
Type 2: *If the company **failed**, we **would lose** all our money.* ➤ 157
Type 3: *If the company **had failed**, we **would have lost** all our money.* ➤ 158

There is another pattern we can call Type 0.
Type 0: *If the company **fails**, we **lose** all our money.* ➤ 156

C The if-clause usually comes before the main clause, but it can come after it.

If you're in a hurry, you needn't wait.
You needn't wait if you're in a hurry.

A comma between the clauses is more likely when the if-clause comes first.

D We can use conditional sentences in different ways: not only to give information but also when we request, advise, criticize, and so on.

Requesting: *If you're going into town, could you post this letter for me, please?*
Advising: *If the headache persists, you should consult a doctor.*
Criticizing: *If you'd remembered your passport, we wouldn't be in such a rush.*
Suggesting: *We can go for a walk if you like.*
Offering: *If you're hungry, help yourself.*
Warning: *If you don't copy the file, you risk losing the information.*
Threatening: *If you don't leave immediately, I'll call the police.*

TIP

The standard types of conditional are not the only possible verb patterns. In general we can use verb forms in the same way as in other sentences. We can say *We've finished, so we can go home*, so we can also say *If we've finished, we can go home*.

156 Type 0 and 1 conditionals

A Type 0 is *if ... + present ... + present*.
*If the doorbell **rings**, the dog **barks**.*
*The batteries **take** over if we **lose** power.*
One thing always follows automatically from another.

Type 0 is also used for the automatic result of a possible future action.
*If we **win** the league, we **get** promoted.*

B Type 1 is *if ... + present ... + will*.
*If it **rains**, we**'ll get** wet.*
*If we **don't hurry**, we **won't be** in time.*
*The milk **will go** off if you **leave** it by the radiator.*
This is an open condition. *If it rains* means that it may or may not rain.

We do not normally use *will* in the if-clause.
NOT ~~If it will rain, ...~~
But we can use *will* in the if-clause for an action happening later than the action in the main clause.
*If this medicine does me / **will do** me good, I'll take it.*

C As well as the present simple, we can use the present continuous or perfect.
*If they**'re having** a party, it'll be noisy.*
*If I**'ve finished** my work by ten, I'll probably watch a film on TV.*

As well as *will*, we can use other modal verbs and similar expressions.

*If they ask me, how **should** I **answer**?*
*I**'m going to look** silly if it all goes wrong.*

We can use the imperative.

*If you make a mistake, **correct** it.*

D A present tense in the if-clause can refer to the present.

*If it**'s raining**, I'm not going out.*
*If you **think** you can do the job, why not apply for it?*

E We can use *will* in the if-clause for willingness and *won't* for a refusal.

*If Tom **will lend** a hand, we'll soon finish.*
*If the car **won't start**, I'll take the bus.*

F Instead of a Type 1 with *if you* + simple present, we can use these patterns in informal speech.

*Touch me **and** I'll scream.*
(If you touch me, I'll scream.)
*Go away **or** I'll scream.*
(If you don't go away, I'll scream.)

TIP

We can use *will* in an if-clause for a request, e.g. *If you**'ll take** a seat, someone will be with you in a moment. If you**'ll** just **sign** here, please. Thank you.*

157 Type 2 conditionals

A Type 2 is *if ... + past ... + would.*
> *If I **had** the money, I **would buy** a yacht.*
> *I'd **tell** you the answer if I **knew** it.*
> *If the plane **wasn't** safe, we **wouldn't fly**.*
> *If we **lived** in the countryside, I'd **have** a longer journey to work.*

The past tense expresses an unreal condition. *If I had the money* means that I haven't really got it, but I am imagining a situation where I have.

We do not normally use *would* in the if-clause.
> NOT *If I would have the money, ...*

B We also use Type 2 for the future.
> *If we **left** early tomorrow, we'd **be** in Manchester by lunch time.*
> *If you **lost** the video, you **would have to pay** for a new one.*

Compare Types 1 and 2.
1: *If we **take** a taxi, it'll be quicker.*
2: *If we **took** a taxi, it'd be quicker.*
Type 1 expresses an open possibility – we may or may not take a taxi.
Type 2 expresses a theoretical possibility – something less real.

Normally we do not mix Types 1 and 2.
> NOT *If you break it, you'd be in trouble.*
> NOT *If you broke it, you'll be in trouble.*

C As well as the past simple, we can use the past continuous or *could*.

*If the sun **was shining**, it'd be perfect.*
*If I **could have** my child looked after, I would go out to work.*

As well as *would*, we can use other modal verbs such as *could* or *might* in the main clause.

*If I had a light, I **could** see.*
*If we could re-start the computer, that **might** solve the problem.*

We can also use continuous forms.

*If Shakespeare was alive today, he **would be writing** for television.*

D We can use *would* in the if-clause for a request.

*If you'**d** just **sign** here, please. Thank you.*
*If you **wouldn't mind** holding the line, I'll try to put you through.*

In a main clause we can use *will* or *can*.

We can also use *would like* in an if-clause, e.g. for a suggestion.

*If you'**d like** to see the exhibition, it would be nice to go together.*

TIP

We can use a Type 2 conditional for a polite request, e.g. *Would it be all right if I brought a friend?* This is less direct and so more polite than *Will it be all right if I bring a friend?*

315

Type 3 conditionals

A Type 3 is *if ...* + past perfect ... + *would* + perfect.

*If you **had come** on your bike, you **would have been** in time.*

*My brother **would have been promoted** if he'd **stayed** in his job.*

*We'd **have gone** to the concert if we'd **known** about it.*

(We **would** have gone if we **had** known.)

The verb forms refer to something unreal, an imaginary past action. *If you had come on your bike* means that really you didn't come on your bike, but I am imagining a situation where you did.

We do not use the past simple or past perfect in the main clause.

*We **would have got** lost if we hadn't bought a map.*

(NOT ~~We had got lost if we hadn't bought a map.~~)

And we do not normally use *would* in the if-clause.

*If you'd **lent** him the money, you would never have got it back.*

(NOT ~~If you would have lent him the money, you would never have got it back.~~)

You may hear clauses such as *if we would have done* in informal speech. But many people regard it as incorrect.

B We can use *could* + perfect in the
if-clause.
*If I **could have warned** you in time,
I would have done.*

As well as *would*, we can use other
modal verbs such as *could* or *might* in
the main clause.
*If I'd written the address down, I **could
have saved** myself a lot of trouble.
The plan **might not have worked** if we
hadn't had a piece of luck.*
We can also use continuous forms.
*If he had had any money, he **wouldn't
have been sleeping** on the streets*

C We can mix Types 2 and 3.
*If Tom really **was** ambitious, he **would
have found** a decent job years ago.
If you **hadn't woken** me up in the
night, I **wouldn't feel** so tired now.*

We can also use a Type 1 condition
with a Type 3 main clause.
*If you **know** London so well, you
shouldn't have got so hopelessly lost.*

TIP

We can use a Type 3 condition to point
out that we were not at fault and to put
the blame on someone else, e.g. *If you
hadn't insisted on taking so much stuff,
we wouldn't have had to pay excess
baggage.*

159 *Should, were, had,* and inversion

The following types of clause are rather formal. It is more usual to use Types 1–3, ▸ 156–158.

A We can use *should* for something that might possibly happen.

*If you **should** fall ill, we will pay your medical expenses.*

*If I **should** be elected, I would do my best to represent your interests.*

More neutral would be *If you fall ill, ...* and *If I was elected ... .*

B Sometimes we use *were* instead of *was*.

*If the picture was/**were** genuine, it would be worth millions of pounds.*

We can also use *were to* for a theoretical possibility.

*If the decision **were to** go against us, we would appeal.*

C In a condition with *should* or *were*, we can invert the subject and verb and leave out *if*.

***Should you** fall ill, we will pay your medical expenses.*

***Should we** not succeed, the consequences would be disastrous.*

***Were the decision** to go against us, we would appeal.*

Were the picture genuine, it would be
worth millions of pounds.
We cannot do this with *was*.
*If the picture **was** genuine, it ...*
(NOT ~~Was the picture genuine, it ...~~)

Compare these sentences.
If I hadn't carried out the order, I
would have lost my job.
Had I not carried out the order, I would
have lost my job.
A Type 3 if-clause has the past perfect
(*If I hadn't carried ...,* ➤ 158). In more
formal English, we can invert the
subject and *had* (*Had I not ...*).

D Look at these examples with *not for.*
*I'd give up teaching **if it wasn't for** the
long holidays.*
(Without the long holidays, I would
give up teaching.)
*You saved my life. **If it hadn't been for**
you, / **Had it not been for** you, I would
have drowned.*
(Without you, I would have drowned.)
We can also use *but for.* ➤ 161B

TIP

We can use *happen to* or *by chance* for
something that is not very probable, e.g.
*If you (should) **happen to** fall ill, you
don't need to worry about the bills,* or
*If by chance you (should) come across a
copy of the book, make sure you buy it.*

160

More about *if*

A *When* and *if*

Compare these sentences.

When Amy comes, can you let her in?
(Amy **will** come.)
If Amy comes, can you let her in?
(Amy **might** come.)

We use *if* (not *when*) for an unreal condition.

If I had a camera, I could take a photo.

In some contexts *when* and *if* are both possible.

*I feel nervous **when/if** I'm flying.*

B *Then*

After an if-clause we can use *then* in the main clause. *Then* emphasizes the link between the two ideas.

*If the figures don't add up, **then** you must have made a mistake.*

C Short clauses

We can sometimes use a short clause with *if* without a subject and verb.

*I'd like a sea view **if** (that is) **possible**.*
*If (you are) **in difficulty**, call this number.*

D *What if*

What if asks you to imagine a situation.

***What if** we can't get tickets?*
***What if** you'd had an accident?*

E *Even if*

Look at this example.

> I'm going to solve this puzzle **even if** it takes me all night.

(It may or may not take me all night, but I'm going to solve it.)

F *Unless*

Unless with a positive verb is equivalent to *if* with a negative verb.

> We'll go broke **unless** we find a sponsor.

(... **if** we do**n't** find a sponsor)

The main clause can be negative.

> You can't play **unless** you're a member.

(You can play **only if** you're a member.)

We do not normally use *unless* meaning *if ... not* in an unreal condition.

> **If** I had**n't** fallen, I would have won.

(NOT *Unless I had fallen, ...*)

And we do not use *unless* when talking about a feeling caused by something not happening.

> I'll be upset **if** you do**n't** come.

(NOT *I'll be upset unless you come.*)

TIP

We can use *what if* to make a suggestion, e.g. **What if** we all meet up this evening?

161 Other ways of expressing a condition

A *As long as, provided*, etc

As well as *if*, we can use *as/so long as* to express a condition.

> *You can smoke **as long as** you do it outside the building.*
> *I don't care what a car looks like **so long as** it gets me from A to B.*

We can also use *provided (that)*, *providing (that)*, and *on condition that*.

> *The machine will last for years **provided (that)** it is looked after properly.*
> *The country was given aid **on condition that** it signed a trade agreement.*

These conjunctions are more formal.

B *In case of, with*, etc

We can use the prepositions *in case of* and *in the event of*.

> ***In case of** fire, break glass.* (on a sign)
> (If there is a fire, ...)
> ***In the event of** a major emergency, local hospitals would be alerted.*
> (If there was a major emergency, ...)

The prepositions *with*, *without*, and *but for* can also express a condition.

> ***With** more time, we could do it properly.*
> (If we had more time, ...)

> **Without** the map, I'd have got lost.
> (If I hadn't had the map, ...)

> **But for** you, I'd have drowned.
> (If it hadn't been for you, ...)

In that case means 'if that is so'.
*I've lost my ticket. ~ **In that case**, you'll have to buy another one.*

Otherwise means 'if that is not so'.
*Hold on tight, **otherwise** you might fall.*

C *In case*

Compare *if* and *in case*.
*I'll get some money from the bank **if** I need some.*
(I'll wait until I need some and then get it.)
*I'll get some money from the bank **in case** I need some.*
(I'll get some now because I might need it later.)

We can use *should* after *in case*.
*I had some water **in case** I woke up / I **should** wake up thirsty in the night.*

We can use *in case* as an adverbial.
*I'll take an umbrella (just) **in case**.*

TIP

In American English *in case* can mean the same as *if*, e.g. **In case** you need any help, let me know.

---

162 Unreal past and subjunctive

A The unreal present and past

After *as if, as though, if, imagine, suppose,* and *supposing,* we can use the past tense for something unreal in the present or something unlikely to happen in the future.

> *Imagine you want/**wanted** to murder someone. How would you go about it?*
> *Suppose we win/**won** the lottery.*

After *it's time* and *would rather,* we do not normally use the present tense.

> *It's time you **had** your hair cut.*
> *I'd rather we all **travelled** together.*

For an unreal situation in the past, we use the past perfect.

> *Suppose you**'d fallen**. What then?*
> *He walked past as if he **hadn't seen** me.*

B The subjunctive

The subjunctive is the base form of a verb. There is no *-s* in the third person singular.

> *We propose that work **go** ahead.*
> *It is important that exact records **be** kept.*

We can use the subjunctive in a that-clause saying that something is necessary. It follows a clause with e.g. *demand, essential, insist, recommend, request, suggest.*

The subjunctive is rather formal and used more in America than in Britain, where other forms are often used.

*We propose that work **should go** ahead.*
*It is important that exact records **are** kept.*

There is a past subjunctive form *were*, which we can use instead of *was* in the first and third person singular.

*If I was/**were** a bit taller, I could reach.*
*Suppose the story was/**were** true.*

We can use it after *as if*, *suppose*, etc.

C Verbs after *wish*

To wish for a future change, we use *would*.

*I wish Simon **would reply** to my emails.*

To wish that the present situation could be different, we use the past or *could*.

*I wish I **had** more spare time.*
(NOT ~~I wish I would have more spare time.~~)
*I wish I **could help**, but I can't.*

For a wish about the past, we use the past perfect or *could* + perfect.

*I wish I'd never **bought** this lousy car.*
*I wish you **could have come** to our party.*

We can use *if only* instead of *I wish*.

***If only** I **had** more spare time.*

TIP

If I were you is useful for giving people advice, e.g. ***If I were you**, I wouldn't worry.*

163 Noun clauses

A A noun clause begins with *that*, a
question word, or *if/whether*.
*I expected **that** there would be problems.*
*The price depends on **where** you sit.*
*We aren't sure **if/whether** we agree.*

In informal English we can often leave
out *that*.
*I knew (**that**) you weren't listening.*

B We use the term 'noun clause' because
these clauses function like noun
phrases. For example, they can be the
object of a sentence.
*I can't believe **you were so stupid**.*
*I wonder **what's happening**.*

Sometimes there is also an indirect
object or a phrase with *to*.
*We told **the driver** we were in a hurry.*
*I mentioned **to Karen** that you would
be here this evening.*

C We sometimes use a noun clause as the
subject of a sentence.
***That you feel upset** is only natural.*
***How we're going to achieve our aim**
hasn't been explained.*
We do not leave out *that* in this
position, and we can use *whether* but
not *if*.
***Whether** we can succeed isn't clear.*

We often prefer to use *it* as subject and put the noun clause at the end.

> *It's only natural **that you feel upset**.*
> *It isn't clear **whether we can succeed**.*

D A noun clause can be a complement of *be*.

> *The truth is **I don't like her much**.*
> *The advantage of this system is **that you get much better picture quality**.*

E A wh-clause or *whether* (but not *if* or *that*) can come after a preposition.

> *They're looking **into what can be done**.*
> *There's no news **on whether the project is going ahead**.*

Sometimes we can leave out a preposition.

> *I was surprised (**at**) how cold it was.*
> *We agreed (**on**) how much we would pay.*

F We can also use a that-clause after some adjectives and nouns.

> *We were **glad things had gone so well**.*
> *What gave you the **idea that I can sing**?*

We normally put in *that* after a noun.

> *The **fact that** I had no ID didn't help.*
> (NOT *The fact I had no ID didn't help.*)

TIP

A that-clause relates to a statement, a wh-clause relates to a wh-question, and a clause with *if/whether* to a yes/no question.

---

164 Nominalization

A Compare these three examples.
Main clause: ***The campaign succeeded,***
and this meant that lives were saved.
Noun clause: *The fact **that the***
***campaign succeeded** meant that lives*
were saved.
Noun phrase: ***The success of the***
***campaign** meant that lives were saved.*

A statement like *The campaign
succeeded* can be a main clause, or we
can use it as a that-clause as part of a
larger sentence. Sometimes we can turn
a clause into a noun phrase such as *the
success of the campaign*. In this case we
change a verb (*succeeded*) into a noun
(*success*). Using a noun phrase rather
than a clause is called 'nominalization'.
It is often neater to use a phrase,
especially in written English.

Here are some more examples.
***The residents' protests** were ignored.*
(The residents protested.)
***The publication of the report** was
delayed for several weeks.*
(The report was published.)

In this example the noun (*beauty*)
corresponds to an adjective
(*beautiful*).
*We love **the beauty of the landscape**.*
(The landscape is beautiful.)

B When we change a clause into a noun phrase, the subject of the clause has the possessive form or comes in an of-phrase. ➤ 86C

I was happy.	Nothing could spoil **my happiness.**
The President departed.	**The President's departure / The departure of the President** was delayed.
The game ended.	I didn't see **the end of the game.**

C A verb + object becomes a noun + preposition + object.

They opened the leisure centre.	The opening **of** the leisure centre was widely welcomed.
Someone attacked the army post.	The attack **on** the army post took place yesterday.
They've changed the law.	There's been a change **in** the law.

The most common preposition after a noun is of.

D An adverb in a clause is equivalent to an adjective in a noun phrase.

The residents protested **angrily.**	The residents' **angry** protests were ignored.
The landscape is **amazingly** beautiful.	Discover the **amazing** beauty of the landscape.

165

Basics of indirect speech

A We use direct speech when we quote someone's words.

> *'I'll ring you later,' said Jack.* (in a story)
> *'This play really made me laugh.' – The Post* (an advertisement for a play)

In 'indirect speech' or 'reported speech' we report the meaning in our own words and from our own point of view.

> *Jack said **he would ring later**.*
> *One critic claims **the play is very funny**.*

The indirect speech is the object of the verbs of reporting *said* and *claims*.

B We can use a verb of reporting with a that-clause or a wh-clause.

> *Polly **said that** she was going away.*
> *He **wondered why** it was so quiet.*

Verbs of reporting are verbs like *agree, ask, believe, hear, know, suggest, think, understand*.

We often use *that* in indirect speech, but in informal English we can leave it out, especially after a common verb like *say*.

> *Alice says (**that**) she'll be five minutes.*

C We can sometimes use a to-infinitive clause or a gerund clause. ➤ 170

> *Jack promised **to ring later**.*
> *Someone suggested **going for a walk**.*

D Sometimes there is an indirect object after the verb of reporting.

> No one **told me** you were coming.
> The police have **warned the public** that the man is dangerous.

Other verbs in this pattern are: *advise, assure, inform, promise, reassure, remind.*

Sometimes we use a phrase with *to*.

> Can you **explain to me** what's going on?
> I **suggested to the others** that we should meet them here.

Other verbs in this pattern are: *admit, announce, complain, declare, mention, point out, recommend, report, say, write.*

E We sometimes use an adjective such as *sure* or *certain* to introduce indirect speech.

> He's **sure** (that) the figure is wrong.

F When reporting two or more sentences, we do not need a verb of reporting in every one.

> The President **said** that the situation was under control. He had sent in the army.

The second sentence is indirect speech.

TIP

As well as speech or writing, we can also report thoughts, e.g. *I thought I had plenty of time, but I only just made it.* The thought is not necessarily expressed in speech.

166

Tell, *say*, and *ask*

A We normally use an indirect object after *tell*.

> You **told me** you didn't like Chinese food.
> Josh **told us** he was going to London.
> (NOT ~~Josh told he was going to London.~~)

But after *say* we do not use an indirect object.

> You **said** you didn't like Chinese food.
> Josh **said** he was going to London.
> (NOT ~~Josh said us he was going to London.~~)

B We can use either a that-clause or a wh-clause after *tell* or *say*.

> Kate **told me** (**that**) she's fed up.
> Kate **said** (**that**) she's fed up.
> Kate **told me what** the matter was.

Say + wh-clause is used mostly in a negative statement or a question where the information is not actually reported.

> Kate **didn't say what** the matter was.
> **Did** they **say how much** it would cost?

C There are a few expressions where we can use *tell* without an indirect object.

> He likes **telling stories** / **telling jokes**.
> Don't **tell lies**. You should **tell the truth**.
> The children learn to **tell the time**.
> Can you **tell the difference** between tap water and bottled water?

D After *say* we can use a phrase with *to*.
 *I **said to him**, 'I've been mugged.'*
 In indirect speech we prefer these
 patterns.
 *I **said** I'd been mugged.*
 *I **told him** I'd been mugged.*
 But we can use a phrase with *to* if the
 information is not reported.
 *The PM **said** a few words **to** the visitors.*
 *What did the boss **say to** you?*

E We use *talk* and *speak* to say who spoke,
 to whom, for how long, or what about.
 *Daniel was **talking** to a young woman.*
 *The President **spoke** for an hour.*
 *We don't **talk** about politics.*
 Talk and *speak* are not verbs of reporting.
 *Laura **said** she was tired.*
 (NOT ~~Laura talked/spoke she was tired.~~)

F We can use *ask* with or without an
 indirect object.
 *Simon looked upset, so I **asked (him)** if
 there was anything wrong.*

 We use *tell* and *ask* in indirect orders
 and requests. ➤ 170A
 *We **told/asked** Mike to hurry up.*

TIP

Remember that you *say something*,
but you *tell somebody something*.

---

167 Changes in indirect speech

A People, place, and time

Imagine a situation where Oliver and Tina are at home one afternoon. Tina wants to go out in the car, but it won't start. She rings the garage and asks a mechanic if he can come and repair it. He is too busy to come immediately, but he agrees to come the next morning. He says:

OK, I'll be at your house at eight tomorrow morning.

A moment later Tina says to Oliver:
The mechanic says he'll be here at eight tomorrow morning.
Now the speaker is a different person, so where the mechanic said *I'll be ...*, Tina says *He'll be ... .* And the speaker is in a different place, so *at your house* for the mechanic is *here* for Tina.

Next day the mechanic has not arrived even by nine o'clock, so Tina rings him and says:
You said you would be here by eight this morning.
Now the time has changed. Instead of *tomorrow morning*, Tina says *this morning.* And the promise is now out of date, so *will* changes to *would.* For changes to verb forms, ➤ 168.

B Pronouns and possessives

When you report what someone has said, both pronouns and possessives can change.

'I'm really enjoying myself.' →
*Jade said **she** was enjoying **herself**.*
'I like your new hairstyle.' →
*Martin said **he** liked **my** new hairstyle.*

C Adverbials of time

Here are some typical changes from direct to indirect speech.

now → *then / at that time / immediately*
today → *yesterday / that day /
on Tuesday,* etc
yesterday → *the day before /
the previous day / on Monday,* etc
tomorrow → *the next day /
the following day / on Thursday,* etc
this week → *last week / that week*
last year → *the year before /
the previous year / in 2005,* etc
next month → *the month after /
the following month / in May,* etc
an hour ago → *an hour before /
an hour earlier / at 2.30,* etc

TIP

Except when we talk about time, *this* or *that* usually changes to *the* in indirect speech, or the phrase is replaced by *it*, e.g. *This steak is nice.* → *She said **the** steak was nice. / She said **it** was nice.*

168

Tenses in indirect speech

A We can use a present-tense verb of
reporting to report recent statements.
*Robert **says** he's hungry.*
In this case we do not change the tense.
I'm hungry. → *He says he's hungry.*

B A verb of reporting is often in a past
tense, even when we report recent
statements.
*He **said** he was hungry.*
We often change the tense in indirect
speech from present to past.
I'm hungry. → *He said he **was** hungry.*

C In general we are more likely to
change the tense if we are unsure if the
statement is still true and still relevant.
*You told me he **lived** in Bath, but actually
he lives in Bristol.* (untrue statement)
*The forecast said it **was** going to rain,
and it did.* (forecast now out of date)

The past tense is also used to report in
a neutral or objective way.
*The PM said it **was** the right decision.*

D The tense change in indirect speech is
from present to past.
'I feel awful.' → *She said she **felt** awful.*
'You're crazy.' → *He thought I **was** crazy.*
'I've got time.' → *I said I **had** time.*

If the verb phrase is more than one word, then the first word changes.

'You're lying.' → I knew she **was** lying.
'I've finished.' → He said he'**d** finished.

So the present continuous changes to the past continuous, and so on.

E A past-tense verb usually changes to the past perfect.

*'I **won** the game.'* → He said he'**d** won.

But *He said he won* is also possible.

A past perfect verb does not change.

F *Will*, *can*, and *may* change to *would*, *could*, and *might*.

'We'll be late.' → I thought we'**d** be late.
*'I **can't** see.'* → He said he **couldn't** see.

Must can be the same or change to *have to*.

*'I **must** go now.'* → Sarah said she **must** go / she **had to** go.

Would, *could*, *should*, *might*, *ought to*, *had better*, and *used to* do not change.

*'I **could** help.'* → He said he **could** help.

TIP

Changing the tense after *said*, *told me*, etc is always possible, while keeping it the same can be a mistake. So in general it is safer to change the tense.

169 Reporting questions

A When we report a question, we use verbs such as *ask, enquire, need to find out, want to know, wonder.*

We can report a wh-question.
'**Where** did you eat?' → I **asked** Elaine **where** she'd eaten.
'**How much** is a ticket?' → James **enquired how much** a ticket was.
'**Who** have you invited?' → Peter is **wondering who** we've invited.
'**When** is the lecture?' → Someone **wants to know when** the lecture is.
'**What** size do you take?' → The assistant **asked** me **what** size I took.

To report a yes/no question, we use *if/whether.*
'Is the drug safe?' → People are **asking if/whether** the drug is safe.
'Has the car been repaired?' → He **wants to know if/whether** the car has been repaired.

After *if/whether* we can use *or not* to stress the need for a yes/no answer.
We need to find out **if/whether** the drug is safe **or not**.
We need to find out **whether or not** the drug is safe.

B In an indirect question the word order is usually subject + verb, as in a statement.

*I'll ask when **the bus leaves**.*

Compare: ***The bus leaves** at three ten.*
(NOT ~~I'll ask when does the bus leave.~~)

But we can use inversion when the reporting verb comes at the end, as a kind of afterthought.

*When **does the bus leave**, I wonder.*

C In an indirect question the tense can change from present to past in the same way as in a statement. ➤ 168

*'What **do** you **want**?'* → *The man asked what we **wanted**.*

*'**Can** we take photos?'* → *Anna wondered if we **could** take photos.*

D We can use an indirect question form after *say, tell,* etc when we are talking about the answer to a question.

*Did Zoe **say when** she would call?*

*I wish you'd **tell** me **whether** you agree.*

*I haven't been **informed what** time the flight gets in.*

TIP

You can use an indirect question when you approach someone to ask politely for information. *Could you tell me where the lift is, please?* is more polite than just asking *Where is the lift?*

170 Reporting requests, offers, etc

A To report an order or request, we usually use *tell/ask* + object + to-infinitive.

> *'Please wait there.'* → He **told us to wait**.
> *'Could you help us, please?'* → We **asked someone to help** us.

B *Ask* can be with or without an indirect object.

> *'Sit down, please.'* → The boss **asked him to sit** down.
> *'May I sit down?'* → He **asked to sit** down.

C We use *ask for* + noun phrase to report a request to have something.

> *'Can I have a receipt, please?'* → I **asked** (the assistant) **for** a receipt.

To report a request for permission, we use *ask if/whether*.

> Tim **asked if/whether** he could smoke.

D There are many kinds of sentences that we can report with a performative verb like *apologize* or *refuse*, which shows the use of the statement. Here are some patterns with such verbs.

- A single clause

> *'I'm sorry.'* → The man **apologized**.
> *'Mind the wet paint.'* → She **warned** me about the wet paint.

- Verb + to-infinitive
  'I'm not walking.' → *I **refused to walk.***
  'I'll be good.' → *He **promised to be** good.*
  Also: *agree, offer, threaten, volunteer.*
- Verb + object + to-infinitive
  'Would you like to come with us?' →
  *They **invited me to go** with them.*
  Also: *advise, remind, warn.*
- Verb + gerund
  'Let's discuss this.' → *He **suggested**
  discussing the matter.*
  Also: *admit, deny.*
- Verb + preposition + gerund
  'I must go.' → *He **insisted on going.***
  'You should have complained.' → *Carl*
  criticized** me **for not complaining.
  Also: *apologize for, object to; accuse ...
  of, congratulate ... on, thank ... for.*
- Verb + that-clause
  'Yes, it's too risky.' → *He **agreed (that)**
  it was too risky.*
  Many verbs can be used in this pattern,
  e.g. *complain, deny, predict, warn.*
- Verb + object + that-clause
  'You'll be fine.' → *They **assured me
  (that)** I would be fine.*
  Also: *promise, reassure, remind, warn.*

TIP

We can also use the form of an indirect
statement or question to report requests,
offers, etc, e.g. *He **said** he would be
good. We **asked** if he could help us.*

171 Basics of relative clauses

A Relative pronouns

A relative clause follows a noun phrase. The clause identifies which one, or it adds information. A relative pronoun (e.g. *who*, *which*, *that*) replaces a personal pronoun.

> The boy **who** won got a prize.
> (NOT ~~the boy who he won~~)
> The film **that** we saw was really good.
> (NOT ~~the film that we saw it~~)

We can sometimes use a clause without a relative pronoun. ➤ 172E

> The film **we saw** was really good.

B Commas with relative clauses

Some clauses are separated from the rest of the sentence by one or two commas and by a short pause in speech.

> Arsenal**, who are third,** play at Chelsea.

This clause adds information about Arsenal. The sentence would make sense without it.

A clause without commas or pause usually identifies which one we mean.

> The team **that Chelsea face** is Arsenal.

The team is Arsenal on its own would not make sense.

C Types of relative clause

There are five functions that relative clauses can perform.

- Identifying clause

  A relative clause without commas can identify which one we mean. ➤ B

  *Who was the man **who said hello?***

- Classifying clause

  A relative clause without commas can say what kind of thing we are talking about.

  *We're looking for a pub **that serves food**.*

  The clause *that serves food* describes the kind of pub we mean.

- Clause used for emphasis

  We can use a relative clause without commas in a pattern with *it + be*. ➤ 25C

  *It's my husband **who does the cooking**.*

- Adding clause

  A relative clause with commas can add more information. ➤ B

  *I was with Ted**, who lives upstairs**.*

- Connective clause

  A relative clause with a comma can tell us what happened next.

  *I shouted to the man**, who ran off**.*

  In speech we use two main clauses.

  *I shouted to the man**, and he** ran off.*

TIP

Sometimes a relative clause is separated from the noun it relates to, e.g. ***The bus was leaving that we wanted to catch***. But in writing you should put the clause next to the noun e.g. ***The bus that we wanted to catch*** was leaving.

343

172 Relative clauses without commas

A *Who, which,* and *that*

We use *who/that* for people and *which/that* with other nouns.

*I know the woman **who/that** served us.*
*It was a dream **which/that** came true.*

With people, *who* is more usual than *that*, especially in writing. After other nouns, *which* can be a little formal.

That is more usual than *which* after a quantifier or pronoun.

*There was **little that** we could do to help.*
*There's **something that**'s worrying me.*

B Relative patterns

The relative pronoun can be the subject or object of the clause.

*I don't like people **who smoke** at work.*
Subject: **They smoke** at work.
*They're the people **that we saw** earlier.*
Object: **We saw them** earlier.

We can often leave out an object relative pronoun. ➤ E

C *Whom*

Who can be an object pronoun.

*I met a friend **who** I knew at college.*

We can also use *whom* as an object.

*I met a friend **whom** I knew at college.*

But *whom* is formal and rather old-fashioned. In everyday speech we use *that* or leave out the pronoun. For more examples of *whom*, ➤ D and ➤ 173B.

D Relatives and prepositions

Who, *which*, and *that* can be the object of a preposition.

*Tom is the man **who** I share a flat **with**.*
(I share a flat **with Tom**.)
*Such is the world **that** we live **in**.*
(We live **in the world**.)

In informal English the preposition comes in the same place as in a main clause, e.g. after *I share a flat* or *we live*.

In more formal English, we can put the preposition before *whom* or *which*.

*the person **with whom** I share a flat*
*factors **over which** we have no control*

E Leaving out the pronoun

We can leave out the pronoun from a clause without commas when it is not the subject.

*It's the hottest summer **I can remember**.*
*The person **we spoke to** was helpful.*

We do not leave out a subject pronoun.
NOT ~~The person spoke to us was helpful.~~

TIP

As a general rule, use *who* for people and *that* with other nouns. Say *the man **who** phoned* but *the bus **that** came*.

345

173 Relative clauses with commas

A A relative clause with commas adds information or says what happens next.

*The President, **who was visiting a local high school,** faced protests by students.*

*She kicked the ball, **which flew over the fence into the next garden.***

Adding clauses and connective clauses are rather formal and typical of a written style.

B The relative clause is separated from the main clause by commas, dashes, or brackets.

*First to shoot was Ali, **who missed**.*

*We live in Parma, **which isn't far away**.*

*The head teacher is Mr Baxter – **whom everyone likes**.*

*The cat (**whose name was Molly**) was sitting on the sofa.*

In an adding clause we use *who*, *whom*, *whose*, or *which* but not *that*. And we cannot leave out the relative pronoun.

C A preposition can go before the relative pronoun.

*The actress thanked her parents, **to whom** she owed her success.*

*I made a call, **for which** I had to pay.*

Putting it at the end is less formal.

*I made a call, **which** I had to pay **for**.*

We can also use a preposition + *which*
+ noun.

> *We got home at midnight, **by which
> time** everyone else was in bed.*

D We can use a quantifier such as *all,
one*, or *some* with *of whom* / *of which*
for a whole or part quantity.

> *There were two people in the car, **one of
> whom** was injured.*
> (**One of them** was injured.)
> *The police received several bomb
> warnings, **all of which** were false
> alarms.*

E *Which* can relate to a whole clause, not
just to a noun.

> *The team lost, **which** wasn't surprising.*
> (**The fact that** the team lost wasn't
> surprising.)
> *We had to wait, **which** annoyed us.*
> *I get paid a bit more now, **which** means
> I can afford to run a car.*

We cannot use *what*.

> NOT ~~The team lost, what wasn't
> surprising.~~

TIP

Adding clauses are not often used in
everyday speech. Use main clauses with
and or *but*, e.g. *The head teacher is Mr
Baxter, **and** everyone likes him. I made
a call, **but** I had to pay for it.*

174

Whose, *what*, and *whoever*

A *Whose*

Whose has a possessive meaning.
> *We helped some people **whose car** broke down.* (**Their car** broke down.)

We use *whose* + noun (*whose car*).
NOT *people whose the car broke down*

Whose + noun can also be the object of the clause or of a preposition.
> *The prize goes to the contestant **whose performance** the viewers like best.*
> *The neighbour **whose dog** I'm looking after is in Australia.*

We can use *whose* with a comma.
> *The ball fell to Rooney, **whose shot** hit the post.*

As well as people, *whose* can refer to human activity or organization.
> *She sang a **song, whose** sentiments moved the audience.*
> *It's the poor **countries whose** exports are earning less money.*

Instead of *whose* relating to a thing, we can use *the* + noun + *of which*.
> *She sang a song, **the sentiments of which** moved the audience.*
> *Look up any word **the meaning of which** is unclear.*

B *What*

We can use *what* in this pattern.

*Let's write a list of **what** we need to pack.*
(**the things that** we need to pack)
I was looking for a coat, but I couldn't find what I wanted. (**the thing that** I wanted)

But *what* cannot relate to a noun.
NOT ~~the coat what I wanted~~

For *what* used for emphasis, ➤ 25D.
***What** I wanted was a coat.*

C *Whoever, whatever,* etc

We can use *whoever, whatever, whichever, wherever,* and *whenever* in a relative clause.

***Whoever** painted this graffiti should clean it off.* (**the person who** painted it – no matter who it is)
*I'll spend my money on **whatever** I like.* (**the thing that** I like – no matter what it is)
***Wherever** he goes, he gets recognized.* (in **the place** he goes – no matter where)

TIP

We cannot use *who* in the same way as *whoever*. We say ***Whoever** designed this building ought to be shot* and not ~~Who designed this building ought to be shot~~. But we can say ***The person who** designed this building ...*

349

175 Relative adverbs

A There are relative adverbs *where*, *when*, and *why*.

*The house **where** I used to live has been knocked down.*

*Do you remember the time **when** we all went to a night club?*

*The reason **why** we can sell so cheaply is because we buy in bulk.*

We use *where* after nouns like *place, area, town, country, house, situation.* We use *when* after nouns like *time, day, weekend, moment, period.* And we use *why* after *reason.*

B We can use *where* and *when* without a noun.

*This is **where** I used to live.*
(**the place where** I used to live)

*Remember **when** we went to a club?*
(**the time when** we went to a club)

C Instead of a clause with *where*, we can use these patterns.

*This is the house **in which** I used to live.*
*This is the house **that** I used to live **in**.*
*This is the house I used to live **in**.*

The pattern with *in which* is rather formal. In informal English *the house I used to live in* is more usual.

Instead of *when* or *why*, we can use this pattern.

*Do you remember the time (**that**) we all went to a night club?*
*The reason (**that**) we can sell so cheaply is because we buy in bulk.*

D Clauses with *when* or *where* can be separated off by commas.

*We walked up to the top of the hill, **where** we got a marvellous view.*
*I'd rather go next week, **when** I won't be so busy.*

We do not leave out *where* or *when* here, and we do not use *that*.

E With the noun *way*, we can use these patterns.

*I hate the **way in which** these adverts pop up on the screen.*
*I hate the **way that** these adverts pop up on the screen.*
*I hate the **way** these adverts pop up on the screen.*

The way in which is more formal.

We can also use *how*.

*I hate **how** these adverts pop up on the screen.*

TIP

Remember it's *the place where*, *the time when*, and *the reason why*.

---

176 Relative clauses with a participle or infinitive

A Active participles

We can use an active participle in a shortened relative clause.

*Who are those people **taking** photos?*
(those people **who are taking** photos)
*He ignored the phone **ringing** on his desk.* (the phone **that was ringing**)

The participle can refer to a state.
*Money **belonging** to the club was stolen.*
(money **that belonged** to the club)
We can also use it to report a message.
*There's a sign **warning** of the danger.*

We can sometimes use the participle for a repeated action.
*People **travelling** into London every day are used to the hold-ups.*
(people **who travel** into London)
But we do not use it for a single action.
*The man **who escaped** has been caught.*
(NOT *The man escaping…*)

B Passive participles

We can use a passive participle in a shortened relative clause for both single and repeated actions.
*This is the design **chosen** for the logo.*
(the design **which has been chosen**)
*Cars **left** here will be towed away.*
(cars **which are left** here)

C Word order with participles

A participle can go before a noun. ➤ 80
*We heard **running** water.*

A participle clause comes after the noun.
*We heard water **running** in the pipes.*
(NOT *We heard running in the pipes water.*)

D Infinitive relative clauses

We can use a relative clause with a
to-infinitive after *first*, *second*, etc;
after *next*, *last*, and *only*; and after a
superlative adjective (e.g. *oldest*).
*Who was the **first** woman **to fly** around
the world?* (the first woman **who flew** ...)
*You're the **only** person **to volunteer**.*
*He became the **youngest** player **to
represent** his country.*

We can use a to-infinitive in this
pattern with a preposition + *which*.
*I need a piano **on which to practise**.*
*It's an ideal location **from which to
explore** the Lake District.*
In less formal English we leave out *which*
and put the preposition at the end.
*I need a piano **to practise on**.*

TIP

The to-infinitive is sometimes used in
quiz questions, e.g. *Which was the first
country **to win** the football World Cup?*

177 Endings: *-s*, *-ed*, and *-y*

A The *-s/-es* ending

We add *-s* for a regular noun plural or the simple third person singular.

rooms games words looks opens

After a sound like *s*, *z*, or *ch*, we add *-es*.
kisses watches bushes taxes
But if the word ends in *e*, we just add *-s*.
places supposes prizes

The *-s/-es* ending is pronounced /s/ after a voiceless sound, /z/ after a voiced sound, and /ɪz/ or /əz/ after *s*, *sh*, etc.
Voiceless: *hopes* /ps/   *fits* /ts/
Voiced: *rides* /dz/   *days* /eɪz/
After *s, sh*, etc: *uses* /zɪz/   *edges* /dʒɪz/

The possessive form of a noun is pronounced in the same way.
Mike's /ks/   *Tina's* /əz/   *the boss's* /sɪz/

B The *-ed/-d* ending

Most regular verbs simply add *-ed*.
played walked seemed offered filled
If the verb ends in *e*, we just add *-d*.
moved continued pleased smiled
For consonant changes with *-ed*, ► 178B.

The *-ed/-d* ending is pronounced /t/ after a voiceless sound, /d/ after a voiced sound, and /ɪd/ after /t/ or /d/.

Voiceless: *jumped* /pt/   *wished* /ʃt/
Voiced: *robbed* /bd/   *played* /eɪd/
/t/ or /d/: *waited* /tɪd/   *landed* /dɪd/

C Consonant + *y*

When a word ends in a consonant + *y*,
the *y* changes to *ie* before *s*.
  study → *studies*   *country* → *countries*

Before most other endings, including
the -ed form and comparative and
superlative forms, the *y* changes to *i*.
  study → *studied*   *silly* → *sillier*
  lucky → *luckily*   *happy* → *happiness*

We do not change *y* after a vowel.
  day → *days*   *buy* → *buyer*
But *pay*, *lay*, and *say* have irregular
forms *paid*, *laid*, and *said* /sed/. Note
also *day* → *daily*.

We keep *y* before *i*.
  copy → *copying*   *lobby* → *lobbyist*

We change *ie* to *y* before -*ing*.
  die → *dying*   *lie* → *lying*

TIP

Most nouns ending in *o* add -*s* in the
plural in the normal way, e.g. *discos,
kilos, photos, pianos, radios, studios,
zoos*. But a few add -*es*, e.g. *echoes,
heroes, potatoes, tomatoes*.

178

Endings with *e* and double consonants

A Leaving out *e*

We often leave out *e* before an ending that starts with a vowel, e.g. *-ing*, *-ize*, *-able*, *-al*.

make → *making*   *private* → *privatize*
love → *lovable*   *culture* → *cultural*

But we keep a double *e* before *-ing*.
see → *seeing*

When we add *-ed*, *-er*, or *-est* to a word ending in *e*, we do not write a double *e*.
type → *typed*   *late* → *later*   *nice* → *nicest*

Some words ending in *ce* or *ge* keep the *e* before *a* or *o*.
noticeable   courageous

We do not usually leave out *e* before a consonant.
move → *moves*   *nice* → *nicely*
Exceptions are words ending in *ue*.
argue → *argument*   *true* → *truly*

To form an adverb from a word ending in a consonant + *le*, we change the *e* to *y*.
simple → *simply*   *possible* → *possibly*
Note also that after *-ic*, we add *-ally*.
dramatic → *dramatically*
An exception is *publicly*.

B The doubling of consonants

Doubling happens in a one-syllable word ending in a single vowel + single consonant.

win → *winner*   *put* → *putting*
big → *biggest*   *plan* → *planned*

We double the consonant before an ending with a vowel. We also double it before *y*.

fog → *foggy*   *Tom* → *Tommy*

We do not double in these cases.

- *y, w,* or *x*.
  stay → *staying*   *slow* → *slower*
- when there are two consonants together
  work → *working*   *hard* → *harder*
- when there are two vowels together
  keep → *keeping*   *broad* → *broadest*

When a word has more than one syllable, we double only if the last syllable is stressed, e.g. *forGET*.

forget → *forgetting*   *prefer* → *preferred*

We do not usually double a consonant in an unstressed syllable.

open → *opening*   *enter* → *entered*

But we double *l* and sometimes *p*.

travel → *travelled*   *jewel* → *jeweller*
handicap → *handicapped*

Americans keep a single *l*, e.g. *jeweler*.

TIP

Remember *tap* → *tapping* and *tape* → *taping*.

Weak forms

A Some grammatical words such as auxiliary verbs, pronouns and prepositions have weak forms in unstressed syllables.

*We'll see you **at** two thirty.*

Here *will* has a written short form *'ll* and a spoken weak form /l/. *At* has a weak form /ət/.

We use the strong forms /wɪl/ and /æt/ in a stressed syllable or when speaking slowly and deliberately.

*Will you be ready in time? ~ I think I **will**.*

*What are you looking **at**?*

On the opposite page there is a list of weak forms.

B *That* can have a weak form /ðət/ when it is a conjunction or relative pronoun.

*I know **that** it's me **that**'s to blame.*

As a demonstrative *that* /ðæt/ does not have a weak form.

*I've read **that** book.*

There as subject has a weak form pronounced /ðə(r)/.

***There**'s a problem.*

There meaning 'in that place' does not have a weak form. It is pronounced /ðeə(r)/.

*The exit is over **there**.*

C These are the main weak forms and their pronunciation.

a /ə/	has /həz/, /əz/, or /z/	some /səm/ or /sm/ ➤ 108C
am /əm/ or /m/	he /hi/ or /i/	than /ðən/
an /ən/	her /hə(r)/ or /ə(r)/	that /ðət/ ➤ B
are /ə(r)/	him /ɪm/	the /ðə/ or /ði/ ➤ 95B
as /əz/	his /ɪz/	them /ðəm/ or /əm/
at /ət/	is /z/	there /ðə(r)/ ➤ B
be /bi/	me /mi/	to /tu/ or /tə/
been /bɪn/	must /məst/ or /məs/	was /wəz/
can /kən/ or /kn/	not /nt/	were /wə(r)/
could /kəd/	of /əv/ or /v/	will /l/
do /du/ or /də/	shall /ʃəl/ or /ʃl/	would /wəd/, /əd/, or /d/
for /fə(r)/	she /ʃi/	you /ju/ or /jə(r)/
from /frəm/	should /ʃəd/ or /ʃd/	your /jə(r)/
had /həd/, /əd/, or /d/		

180

Short forms

A We often use short forms in informal writing and to represent speech.

*It's the disco tomorrow, **isn't** it?*
I'll see you there.   Who's the DJ?

We use an apostrophe instead of part of a word, e.g. *it's* instead of *it is*. There is no space before the apostrophe.

Most short forms are with auxiliary verbs, pronouns, and question words. But we can sometimes use a noun.

*The **heating'll** soon warm us up.*

We cannot use a short form of a verb when it would be stressed in speech.

*Is it tomorrow? ~ Yes, it **is**.*

But unstressed *n't* can end a sentence.

*Is it expensive? ~ No, it **isn't**.*

B The form *'s* can mean *is* or *has*.

It's a big house. It's got six bedrooms.
(It **is** ... . It **has** got ... .)

And the form *'d* can mean *had* or *would*.

If you'd gone, you'd have enjoyed it.
(If you **had** gone, you **would** have ...)

There are two different ways we can shorten *is not* and *are not*.

*It **isn't** working. / It's **not** working.*
*We **aren't** ready. / We're **not** ready.*

Other forms like *I'll not, I've not* are less usual than *I won't, I haven't*, etc.

C These are the main short forms.

aren't	are not	I'd	I had/would	she's	she is/has	weren't	were not
can't	cannot	I'll	I will/shall	shouldn't	should not	what'll	what will
couldn't	could not	I'm	I am	that's	that is/has	what's	what is/has
daren't	dare not	I've	I have	there'd	there had/would	when's	when is
didn't	did not	isn't	is not	there'll	there will	where's	where is/has
doesn't	does not	it'll	it will	there's	there is/has	who'd	who had/would
don't	do not	it's	it is/has	they'd	they had/would	who'll	who will
hadn't	had not	let's	let us	they'll	they will	who's	who is/has
hasn't	has not	mightn't	might not	they're	they are	won't	will not
haven't	have not	mustn't	must not	they've	they have	wouldn't	would not
he'd	he had/would	needn't	need not	wasn't	was not	you'd	you had/would
he'll	he will	oughtn't	ought not	we'd	we had/would	you'll	you will
he's	he is/has	shan't	shall not	we'll	we will/shall	you're	you are
here's	here is	she'd	she had/would	we're	we are	you've	you have
how's	how is/has	she'll	she will	we've	we have		

Irregular verbs

Base Form	Past Tense	Past Participle
arise	arose	arisen
awake	awoke	awoken
be	was/were	been
bear	bore	borne
beat	beat	beaten
become	became	become
begin	began	begun
bend	bent	bent
bet	bet	bet
bid *(offer money)*	bid	bid
bid *(order)*	bade	bidden
bite	bit	bitten
bleed	bled	bled
blow	blew	blown
break	broke	broken
breed	bred	bred
bring	brought	brought
broadcast	broadcast	broadcast
build	built	built
burn	burnt	burnt
	burned	burned
burst	burst	burst
bust	bust	bust
	busted	busted
buy	bought	bought
cast	cast	cast
catch	caught	caught
choose	chose	chosen
cling	clung	clung
come	came	come
cost	cost	cost

Base Form	Past Tense	Past Participle
creep	crept	crept
cut	cut	cut
deal	dealt	dealt
dig	dug	dug
dive	dived	dived
	dove	
do	did	done
draw	drew	drawn
dream	dreamt	dreamt
	dreamed	dreamed
drink	drank	drunk
drive	drove	driven
dwell	dwelt	dwelt
eat	ate	eaten
fall	fell	fallen
feed	fed	fed
feel	felt	felt
fight	fought	fought
find	found	found
fit	fitted/fit	fitted/fit
flee	fled	fled
fling	flung	flung
fly	flew	flown
forbid	forbade	forbidden
forecast	forecast	forecast
forget	forgot	forgotten
forgive	forgave	forgiven
forsake	forsook	forsaken
freeze	froze	frozen
get	got	got (US: got/gotten)
give	gave	given
go	went	gone/been ➤ 44F

Base Form	Past Tense	Past Participle
grind	ground	ground
grow	grew	grown
hang	hung/hanged	hung/hanged
have	had	had
hear	heard	heard
hit	hit	hit
hold	held	held
keep	kept	kept
kneel	knelt	knelt
	kneeled	kneeled
knit	knit	knit
	knitted	knitted
know	knew	known
lay	laid	laid
lead	led	led
lean	leant	leant
	leaned	leaned
leap	leapt	leapt
	leaped	leaped
learn	learnt	learnt
	learned	learned
leave	left	left
let	let	let
lie	lay	lain
light	lit	lit
	lighted	lighted
lose	lost	lost
make	made	made
mean	meant	meant
meet	met	met
mistake	mistook	mistaken
mow	mowed	mown
		mowed

Base Form	Past Tense	Past Participle
pay	paid	paid
put	put	put
quit	quit	quit
	quitted	quitted
read	read	read
rid	rid	rid
ride	rode	ridden
ring	rang	rung
rise	rose	risen
run	ran	run
say	said	said
see	saw	seen
seek	sought	sought
sell	sold	sold
send	sent	sent
set	set	set
sewed	sewed	sewn
		sewed
shake	shook	shaken
shed	shed	shed
shine	shone	shone
	shined	shined
shoot	shot	shot
show	showed	shown
		showed
shut	shut	shut
sing	sang	sung
sink	sank	sunk
sit	sat	sat
slay	slew	slain
sleep	slept	slept
slide	slid	slid
sling	slung	slung
slink	slunk	slunk

Base Form	Past Tense	Past Participle
slit	slit	slit
smell	smelt	smelt
	smelled	smelled
sow	sowed	sown
		sowed
speak	spoke	spoken
speed	sped	sped
	speeded	speeded
spell	spelt	spelt
	spelled	spelled
spend	spent	spent
spill	spilt	spilt
	spilled	spilled
spin	spun	spun
spit	spat	spat
split	split	split
spoil	spoilt	spoilt
	spoiled	spoiled
spread	spread	spread
spring	sprang	sprung
stand	stood	stood
steal	stole	stolen
stick	stuck	stuck
sting	stung	stung
stink	stank	stunk
stride	strode	stridden
strike	struck	struck
string	strung	strung
strive	strove	striven
swear	swore	sworn
sweep	swept	swept
swell	swelled	swelled
		swollen
swim	swam	swum
swing	swung	swung

Base Form	Past Tense	Past Participle
take	took	taken
teach	taught	taught
tear	tore	torn
tell	told	told
think	thought	thought
thrive	thrived	thrived
	throve	thriven
throw	threw	thrown
thrust	thrust	thrust
tread	trod	trodden
understand	understood	understood
upset	upset	upset
wake	woke	woken
wear	wore	worn
weave	wove	woven
weep	wept	wept
wet	wet	wet
	wetted	wetted
win	won	won
wind	wound	wound
withdraw	withdrew	withdrawn
wring	wrung	wrung
write	wrote	written

Index

INDEX

INDEX

INDEX

378

INDEX

INDEX

Key to symbols

Phonetic symbols

iː	tea	ʊ	book	əʊ	so
ɪ	sit	uː	fool	aʊ	now
i	happy	u	actual	ɔɪ	boy
e	ten	ʌ	cup	ɪə	dear
æ	had	ɜː	bird	eə	chair
ɑː	car	ə	away	ʊə	sure
ɒ	dog	eɪ	pay		
ɔː	ball	aɪ	cry		

p	put	f	first	h	house
b	best	v	van	m	must
t	tell	θ	three	n	next
d	day	ð	this	ŋ	song
k	cat	s	sell	l	love
g	good	z	zoo	r	rest
tʃ	cheese	ʃ	ship	j	you
dʒ	just	ʒ	pleasure	w	will

(r) shows a linking r, pronounced before a
    vowel but (in British English) not before a
    consonant
ˈ precedes a stressed syllable

Other symbols

The symbol / (forward slash) between two words
or phrases means that either is possible.
We also uses slashes around phonetic symbols,
e.g. *tea* /tiː/.
Brackets ( ) around a word or phrase in an
example mean it can be left out.

→ means that two things are related.

~ means that there is a change of speaker.

➤ is a reference to another section where there
    is more information.